AF413712

STEPHEN M. SHAPIRO

YOU'RE NOT PLAYING WITH A FULL DECK

WHY THE COWORKERS WHO DRIVE YOU CRAZY ARE YOUR **UNFAIR ADVANTAGE**

CONTENTS

This isn't just another book or personality test.

It's a complete system for building a culture of innovation and collaboration that delivers breakthrough results.

The system is built around Personality Poker. More than 250,000 professionals have used this card-based assessment to understand how they contribute to and detract from the success of their team.

Before we begin, take the free one-minute assessment at **PersonalityPokerPlay.com**. You'll discover which type of innovator you are, your blind spots, and what you uniquely bring to any team.

While you're there, you'll also find training videos, a graphical summary, a cheat sheet, and options to purchase physical cards or our complete DIY system at a discounted price.

Once you know your hand, come back here and learn how to play it.

It's time to shuffle the deck and deal yourself in.

PersonalityPokerPlay.com

ANTE UP

Start Here: Your Opening Hand

The person who drove me the craziest turned out to be the one who saved my career.

In 1995, while at Accenture, I was asked to lead a massive $30 million project.

Given the size of the assignment, I decided to bring in a co-leader and chose my friend John.

John was a big, jolly, and happy guy. We were two peas in a pod: imaginative, energetic, and people-focused. The chemistry was perfect, and we were sure it would lead to perfect results.

There are three things I can honestly say about this project:

1. We developed brilliant and game-changing ideas.
2. The team had a blast and loved us.
3. It was a colossal waste of $30 million.

John and I were so focused on ideas and people that we forgot we needed to produce something of value.

It was a complete failure. No one on the leadership team cared about structure, deadlines, or execution. We only had people like us.

Then came my next project. Smaller budget. Only $6 million. And this time, I didn't get to pick my co-leader. They gave me Ray.

Ray was a self-proclaimed "anal-retentive program manager." He lived for deadlines and schedules.

Every day he asked, "Where's the deliverable?" "Why are we over budget?" "What's the status?"

He drove me crazy.

One day, I snapped. I pulled him aside for lunch and said, "Ray, I don't like you." Without missing a beat, he said, "Steve, I don't like you either."

We laughed.

Then I said something that changed everything, a realization I had after the $30 million fiasco: "I may not *like* you, Ray. But I *need* you. I failed at my previous project because I didn't have someone like you."

That was the turning point.

For the next three hours, we talked about how we would drive each other crazy, the value each of us would bring, and how we could work together more effectively.

He brought structure and kept me grounded. I brought creativity and loosened him up. Together we made it work.

The result of this deep appreciation and collaboration?

We launched a wildly successful program that was delivered to 20,000 consultants in only nine months, and the impact lasted for years.

We created a movement that transformed the company by getting people to think about innovation and impact, rather than just software and implementation.

That project became one of the proudest achievements of my career. People still talk about it nearly thirty years later.

We succeeded not in spite of our differences, but because of them. It was not because of me. It was because of Ray. The person who drove me crazy turned out to be the ace up my sleeve.

That is when it hit me. Most of us are not playing with a full deck. We are missing the perspectives that matter most.

That experience sparked a question. What if teams could see their differences as strengths from day one?

The Game Behind the Metaphor

To help teams see what's missing, I created Personality Poker in 2005. The system uses a standard deck of playing cards with suits, colors, and numbers. Each card includes a word that reflects a different personality trait: curious, loyal, disciplined, logical.

Most people and most teams aren't playing with a full deck. They're missing critical strong suits: the data-driven analysts, the unconventional thinkers, the disciplined doers, or the empathetic connectors.

This book shows you what you bring to the table, what's missing, and who you need to balance the deck. You'll discover why sameness stifles breakthrough results—and how to work better with people who see the world differently.

You'll start to see yourself, and the people who drive you crazy, in a whole new way.

The same insights that help you understand yourself can transform how you lead, innovate, and build culture.

Designed for Innovation, Not Personalities

People often ask, "Is this like DiSC®, Myers-Briggs®, or CliftonStrengths®?"

Here's the short answer: it's not.

Those tools describe individuals. Personality Poker was built to drive innovation.

Most assessments are mirrors. They show you how you see yourself.

Personality Poker is a map. It reveals your blind spots, who you need on your team, and how to play better together.

I didn't set out to make another personality test. I wanted a tool that helps organizations innovate faster by embracing diversity of thought.

Innovation doesn't happen when everyone thinks alike. It happens when different minds combine productively.

The concepts in Personality Poker go beyond individuals and address team and organizational dynamics. It helps you:

- See how others perceive you
- Build balanced and collaborative teams
- Design more productive, engaging meetings
- Shape cultures that value every kind of thinker
- Identify why growth stalls and how to stimulate innovation
- Sell and market more effectively

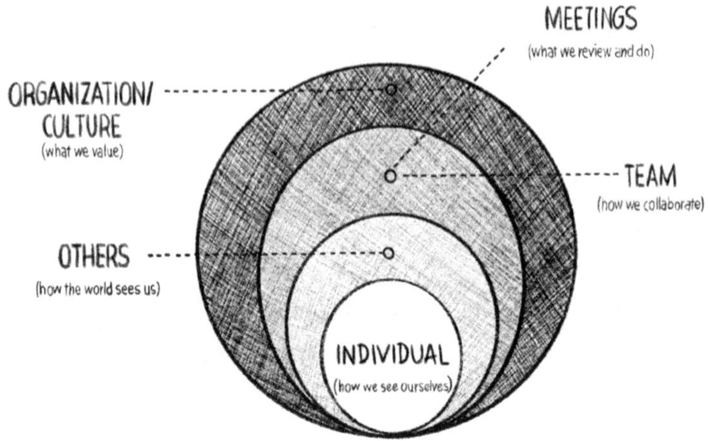

The Five Levels of Personality

As the graphic shows, Personality Poker works at every level, from individual self-awareness to organizational culture.

- **Individual**: Understanding your own strong suits and blind spots
- **Others**: Reading their style and seeing how they read yours
- **Team**: Building balanced teams and managing creative conflict
- **Meetings**: Designing meetings that bring out every suit because meetings have personalities too
- **Organization/Culture**: Shaping environments where all styles thrive and innovation flourishes

Most personality assessments stop at helping you understand yourself. Personality Poker goes further: it diagnoses what's not working within yourself, your team, and your organization so you can create something new and better.

At the organizational level, this means examining which

personalities get hired, promoted, and celebrated—and whether your culture has become too narrow to innovate. It shows you the gaps that hold you back and the combinations that drive you forward.

You don't even need the cards to apply these concepts. Once you understand the process, the principles work.

How This Book Is Structured

This book has three main parts, plus some **Wild Cards**.

Part One helps you understand yourself and how others see you.

Part Two shows you how to build balanced teams, design better meetings, leverage culture, and drive innovation.

Part Three goes deeper into the numbers and combinations that make every hand unique.

The **Wild Cards** are for curious readers who want to know whether Personality Poker is scientifically valid, why blending different experiences generates breakthroughs, and how it applies in an AI-driven world.

Each chapter includes **Put It into Play** action steps to help you apply what you've learned and a **Next Hand** transition to set up what's coming next.

Whether you're part of a team of two or leading thousands, this book will help you play smarter, faster, and with a full deck.

Why We Are Missing the Cards We Need

Why don't most of us play with a full deck?

Decades of research make it clear: opposites don't attract—they detract. They don't pull together; they push apart.

Don't believe me? Think about the people in your life. Your closest friends. The colleagues you click with. The family members who don't drive you crazy.

Be honest. Are they usually like you or different? Most likely, they share your interests, quirks, and personalities.

If opposites really attracted, cat people and dog people would be best friends.

Vegans and bacon lovers would share meals.

Red Sox fans would cheer for the Yankees. You know that's not happening.

We surround ourselves with people who think like us and act like us. It feels good. It's easy.

But in business, it's dangerous.

When you only hire people who "fit the mold," your organization eventually grows mold.

Ideas go stale. Innovation dies.

Sameness feels safe. But it never sparks growth.

The people who drive you crazy may be the ones who complete you. The perspectives you resist may be exactly what you're missing.

This book is about finding those missing cards.

Why This Book Is for You

This book is for anyone who's ever looked around a meeting, a team, or even their own life and thought, "Something or someone is missing."

You might be a leader trying to drive innovation. A manager trying to build a stronger culture. Or an individual who just wants to feel energized at work again.

No matter your role, this is about seeing yourself and others more clearly. It's about creating environments where every style has a place and every voice is heard and appreciated.

You'll learn how to leverage differences for better results. How to make teams click. How to build a culture where innovation isn't a buzzword, it's a habit.

You don't need another personality test. You need a way to play with a full deck. To see what's missing, to value the gaps, and use these insights to grow.

That's what this book is about.

Before diving in, go to PersonalityPokerPlay.com to play the online version and get your hand.

We succeeded not in
spite of our differences,
but because of them.
To win big in business,
you need to play
with a full deck.

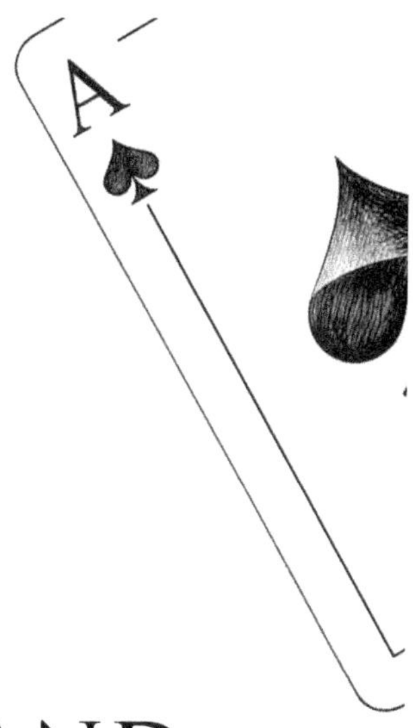

PART ONE

DEAL YOUR HAND

How You See Yourself and How Others See You

Like in poker, you can't play the game until you know your cards.

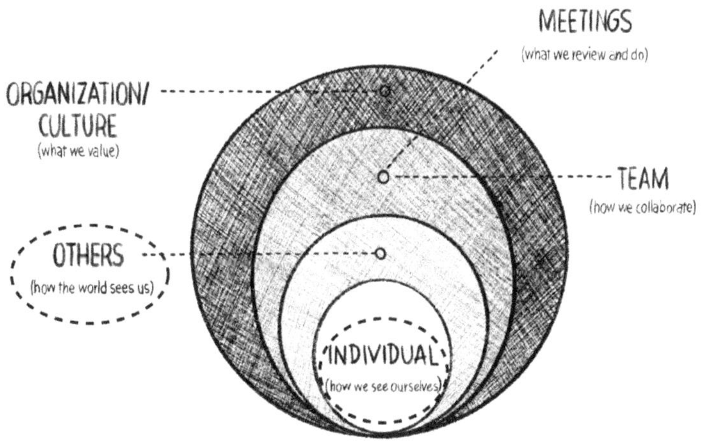

Part One focuses on the first two levels: understanding yourself (Individual) and how others see you (Others).

You'll discover which suit best fits your personality, explore whether it's innate or learned, and understand why knowing who you *are not* is just as important as knowing who you are.

You'll also learn how others read your "tells" and how to recognize strong suits in others.

Once you know your cards, you can finally play to your best hand and win with authenticity.

WHAT SUITS YOU?

The Four Personalities You Can't Win Without

Like every deck of cards, Personality Poker has four suits. Each one represents a completely different way of thinking and working. Each one is essential.

~~~~~~~~~~~~~~~~~~

We start with the suits. The four suits connect to the four steps of the innovation process that we explore in Chapter 12.

Each suit represents a unique way of seeing the world. Each is essential—and some might drive you crazy.

- ♠ Some tackle challenges with analysis (Spades)
- ♦ Others with imagination (Diamonds)
- ♣ Some focus on plans and action (Clubs)
- ♥ Others on human connection (Hearts)

No single suit wins the game on its own.
~~~~~~~~~~~~~~~~~~

It's time to explore the four suits.

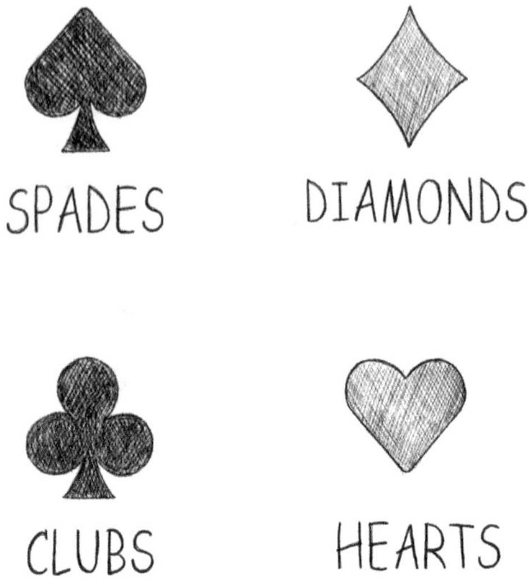

The Four Suits

♠ Spades want the facts

Spades are driven by logic and precision; they look for proof in every decision. Realistic and detail-oriented, they thrive on complex challenges and demand facts and figures. **Warren Buffett** is a classic Spade, always asking, "What's the evidence?" before making a move.

♦ Diamonds are creative

Diamonds are the visionaries and adventure seekers, fueled by curiosity and driven by ideas. They're drawn to what's new and different. Always chasing the next spark of inspiration, always wondering, "Wouldn't it be cool if…?" **Sir Richard Branson,** founder of the Virgin Group, is a Diamond. Dynamic, imaginative, and wildly creative.

♣ Clubs plan and execute

Clubs are into actions and process. Organized, focused, and relentlessly results-oriented. They execute on ideas and deliver measurable results. They love structure, deadlines, and accountability. They keep teams moving forward, always asking, "Where's the deliverable?" **Jack Welch**, former CEO of GE, is a Club. Goal-oriented, disciplined, obsessed with execution. Ray, my co-leader at Accenture, was also a Club.

♥ Hearts are human connectors

Hearts lead with empathy, thrive on relationships, and bring people together. They value people over processes and connection over checklists. They listen first, care deeply, and nurture the bonds that make great work possible. They ask, "How's everyone doing?" **Oprah Winfrey** is a Heart, thriving on connection, empathy, and lifting people up.

No suit is perfect. Each has strengths. Each has blind spots.

But put them together, and you've got balance. Data. Ideas. Action. People. That's when the magic happens.

You don't need to master all four suits. You just need to know your strong suit and then play with others who bring the cards you don't have.

That's how you play with a full deck.

PUT IT INTO PLAY

Your strong suit is your starting point. Knowing it changes how you see yourself, your team, and your work.

PLAY THE GAME.
If you haven't done so, either use the physical cards or play the free online version (PersonalityPokerPlay.com). Check the results. Does it feel like you? Would you choose a different suit? Go with your gut.

PICK YOUR SUIT.
Don't want to play the game? No problem. Just look at the four descriptions. Which one sounds most like you? Write it down. If you're unsure, ask yourself: "Which description makes me think, 'Yes, that's me'?"

DOES MORE THAN ONE SUIT RESONATE?
It's okay to pick more than one. Most people are a mix of two or three suits, but rarely all four. As you'll discover in Chapter 3, who you are not is more important than who you are.

KEEP IT HANDY.
You'll need your suit for the rest of the book. Write it on a sticky note and put it where you'll see it.

You don't need to
master all four suits.
You just need to know
your strong suit, and
then play with others
who bring the cards
you don't have.

Next Hand: *Once you know your suit, the next question is: are you naturally that way, or did you learn to play that card over time?* →

CHAPTER 2

BORN THIS WAY OR JUST FAKING IT?

Why Natural Strong Suits Beat Learned Skills

You can learn almost anything if you try hard enough. But true strong suits are the traits that give you energy, not the ones that drain you.

A client of mine, David, ran a market research company. Data. Analysis. Facts. He loved spreadsheets.

We played Personality Poker.

Given his role, I assumed he would select primarily Spades.

But I was wrong.

He selected mainly Hearts.

I was confused. How could a data guy pull mainly people cards?

I asked him, "What's your biggest challenge right now?" He said, "Sales." "And what have you been doing most days?" "Selling. Networking. Building relationships."

That's when it clicked. He wasn't really a Heart. He was acting like one.

David had **adapted**. He loved Spade work, but his daily grind forced him into Heart work.

This was an aha moment for him. If he hired natural Hearts to handle sales, he could get back to analysis, the work that energized him.

Natural, Learned, and Aspirational Traits

Some traits are **innate or natural.** You were born with them. They feel easy. They energize you.

Others are **learned.** Picked up along the way. Maybe the job demanded it. Maybe your parents pushed it. Maybe school drilled it in.

Learned traits can fool you. You get good at them. But they drain you.

Then there are **aspirational traits.** The ones you *wish* you had. The cards you'd like people to see. The version of yourself you hope to project.

Here's the danger: Learned and aspirational traits can mask your true strong suits. They can push you into roles that don't fit. They can make you successful on paper but empty inside.

Learned styles aren't bad. They help us flex when needed. They help us grow. But too much time outside your strong suit doesn't just feel uncomfortable. It leads to burnout.

Think of burnout as your personality filing a complaint.

David had been faking it without even knowing it.

Don't let learned skills define you. Don't let aspirational traits distract you. Find the things you were born to do.

That's where your real strength lives.

PUT IT INTO PLAY

Separate what energizes you from what drains you. That's where your true strong suit lives.

 **Energy audit.** If you've played Personality Poker (physical or online), review your cards. Which ones give you energy? Keep those. Which ones drain you? Discard them. Those are learned, not natural.

 **No cards? No problem.** List your top five-to-seven traits. Cross out the ones that exhaust you, even if you're good at them. What's left is the real you.

 **Time box the drain.** When you *must* work outside your natural style, set a focused sixty-minute block for the task. Accept that discomfort is normal.

 **Want to go deeper?** Check out Chapter 18 for a more philosophical look at identity and whether personality changes over time.

Learned and aspirational traits can mask your true strong suits. They can push you into roles that don't fit. They can make you successful on paper, but empty inside.

Next Hand: *Now that you have a better idea of who you really are, not just what you've adapted to become, it's time to uncover one of the most important points of Personality Poker: who you are not.* →

CHAPTER 3

Who You Are Not Is More Important Than Who You Are

Why Identifying Your Gaps Creates Real Clarity

In most Personality Poker sessions, 95 percent of people are missing at least one suit. That's the insight: The suits you lack point to the people you need most.

When I play Personality Poker, I'm mainly a Diamond, with some Spades and Hearts. But Clubs? I never pick those cards. Not one.

Remember Ray, the detail-oriented program manager who completed my hand? Pure Club. I'm the opposite. And that's exactly the point.

Know what drains you and what you'll never love. That's not a weakness to fix—it's an opportunity for collaboration.

The most dangerous phrase in business is "I can handle it."

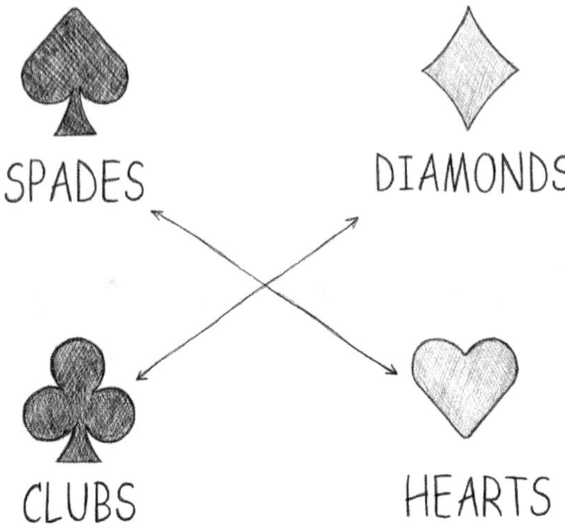

Finding Your Opposite

Finding What's Missing

Knowing who you are not is the fastest way to see who you need by your side.

If you're unsure which suit you're missing, check the graphic. It's often the one diagonally opposite your own.

If you're a **Diamond**, maybe you'll never love rigid processes (Clubs).

If you're a **Spade**, using your gut to make decisions may seem reckless (Hearts).

If you're a **Club**, ambiguity and spontaneity might drive you nuts (Diamonds).

If you're a **Heart**, worrying about data and analytics is probably the last place you want to be (Spades).

You can't be great at everything. If you try, you'll be great at nothing.

When you admit what you're not, you stop trying to cover every base yourself. You start looking for people who complement you, not compliment you. You need people who complete you, not flatter you.

You stop competing with colleagues who are different from you and start appreciating them.

Teams filled with sameness hit walls. Teams with a full deck thrive because everyone knows their role and no one is pretending.

When you know who you are not, you know who you need. And that's where the magic of collaboration begins.

PUT IT INTO PLAY

Knowing who you're *not* is just as powerful as knowing who you are.

 **Identify your missing suits.** Look at the four suits. Which one(s) do you almost never identify with? Write them down.

 **Name what you avoid.** List two tasks you consistently dodge at work. Those reveal your gaps.

 **Stop trying to fix yourself.** Instead of forcing yourself to "get better" at what drains you, find someone who actually enjoys those tasks.

 **Partner up.** Collaborate with someone whose strength is your gap. Watch how both of you win.

A 

 Know what drains
you and what
you'll never love
or be good at. This
is not a weakness.
It's an opportunity
for collaboration.
When you know
who you are
not, you know
who you need. 

A

Next Hand: *Once you've clarified your true self, it's time to read the room. In the next chapter, you'll learn how to recognize others' suits, sometimes before they say a word.* → 

CHAPTER 4

READING THE TELLS

Seeing the Suits Around You

Reading the tells is like playing poker. You might not see someone's cards, but you can still spot their hand if you know what to look for.

I once worked with a manager, Sarah, who was hiring for her team. She wanted people who didn't just fit the mold but brought something different to the table.

She asked me how to do this without using the cards in an interview.

I suggested she ask an open-ended question: "What are you most proud of in your previous job?"

Then I told her to listen carefully, not just to what they said, but how they said it.

Within their answers, she could read their suit: facts and data revealed a Spade, achievements pointed to a Club, creativity and fun signaled a Diamond, and a focus on people meant a Heart.

People rarely hide their style. They announce it. Repeatedly.

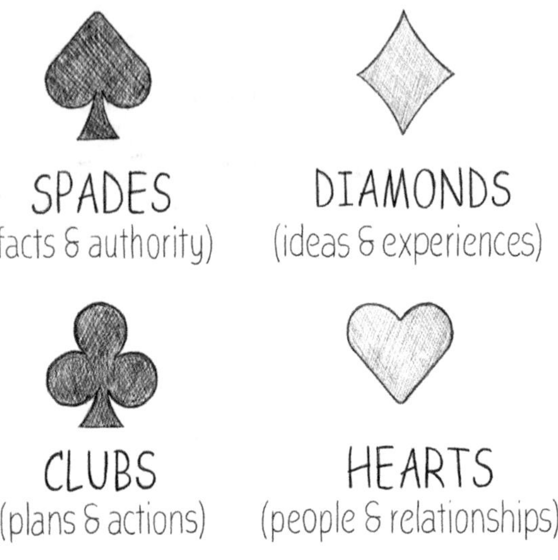

Reading the Four Suits

♠ Spades: Facts and Data

Spades love logic.

Their proudest moments are filled with proof: metrics, analysis, and results backed by evidence. They might say, "The data showed a clear improvement," or, "We studied the data and found the real problem everyone else missed."

They tend to ask clarifying questions like, "How do you measure success?" or, "What evidence do you have to support your belief?"

Their body language is contained and precise. You might see them leaning slightly back with their arms crossed, eyes narrowing as they analyze. Or maybe their chin is resting on their hand in thought.

Their tone is calm and deliberate, revealing a mind sorting through information for patterns and validity.

Picture Rodin's famous statue, *The Thinker*. That's a classic Spade pose. Or imagine arms crossed and a subtle frown: the sign of a more skeptical Spade.

◆ Diamonds: New Ideas and Experiences

Diamonds enjoy talking about what's new and different.

Ask what they're proud of, and they'll get energized describing a project that broke the mold: "We tried something no one else had done," or, "We reimagined the customer experience."

They may ask, "Have you ever thought about doing it this way?" or, "What if we took this idea further?"

Their body language is energetic and expressive.

They gesture as they speak, lean forward with curiosity, eyes widening with excitement. They jump between ideas mid-thought. You can feel their creative pulse in the rhythm of their voice.

♣ Clubs: Plans, Actions, and Results

Clubs focus on outcomes and process.

Their stories center on getting things done: "I led a project that finished ahead of schedule," or, "We hit every target on the list."

They ask pragmatic questions like, "What's the timeline?" or, "How will we achieve the result?"

Their body language shows controlled intensity. Some are methodical: steady, deliberate, and reliable. Others are driven: sitting upright, tapping a pen, checking the clock, eager for action.

A common move is the karate chop: "We did this, then this, then that."

♥ Hearts: People and Relationships

Hearts speak from the heart.

Their proudest moments often involve others: "I helped a teammate grow into a leadership role," or, "Our team came together when it really mattered."

Some Hearts focus on depth and build meaningful connections through attentive listening and steady eye contact.

Others thrive on breadth and are natural networkers who light up when meeting new people.

Their questions always revolve around people: "Who was involved? How did the team feel?" With Hearts, connection is always the point.

Not all Hearts, Clubs, Diamonds, or Spades look the same. Some are steady, others bold; some think deeply, others move fast.

Those differences (which we'll explore in Chapter 15) explain why two people with the same suit can still act so differently.

You don't need the cards to read the room. Observing body language, word choice, and energy helps you understand who you're dealing with and how to connect.

Once you start noticing the tells, you'll spot Spades, Diamonds, Clubs, and Hearts everywhere—long before anyone plays a card.

PUT IT INTO PLAY

You can spot suits without the cards. Just watch, listen, and notice patterns.

 **Pick one person to observe.** In your next meeting, choose someone and watch how they show up. What do they talk about? How do they move? Where does their energy go?

 **Listen for the clues.** Do they reference data and evidence (Spade)? Talk about what's new and different (Diamond)? Focus on deadlines and results (Club)? Ask about people and relationships (Heart)?

 **Watch their body language.** Are they leaning back with their arms crossed (Spade)? Gesturing energetically (Diamond)? Sitting upright and focused on action (Club)? Making warm eye contact and connecting (Heart)?

 **Test your guess.** Ask them an open-ended question like, "What are you most proud of lately?" Their answer will reveal their suit. Or ask directly: "Which suit do you think you are?"

 **Practice everywhere.** The more you read the tells, the faster you'll spot patterns—in meetings, interviews, and casual conversations.

Listen carefully, not just to what they say, but how they say it. Reading the tells helps you understand who you're dealing with and how to connect.

Next Hand: *Now that you can read others, it's time to look at your own cards again. The next chapter shows how others see your hand.* →

CHAPTER 5

THE HAND YOU ARE DEALT

How Others See Us Reveals More Than We Think

We think we're showing people who we really are. But they might be seeing something completely different.

~~~~~~~~~~~~~~~~~~~~~~~~~

I once worked with Rick, a city manager in Texas. When he picked his own cards, he had a flush of Hearts: caring, people-focused, motivational.

But the cards his team gave him were all Clubs: disciplined, process-driven, a manager's manager.

That was their reality, not his truth.

Although his title was that of a manager, he didn't enjoy the heavy process work. He wanted to inspire and connect.

So he made a change: he told everyone what energized him, then shifted some of the Club tasks to others.
~~~~~~~~~~~~~~~~~~~~~~~~~

The result? He reduced stress, became more effective, and helped his team see who he really was.

Understanding the gap between how he saw himself and how others saw him changed everything.

You can discover this same disconnect without cards. Just ask your team to describe how they see you, then notice where their answers surprise you.

Remember, most feedback isn't wrong. It just might not be what we want to hear.

People Don't See You the Way You See Yourself

Research shows why this matters: your self-perception and others' perception line up only 50 percent of the time.

Neither view is fully accurate. It's only by comparing both that we get the real picture.

Some traits are easy to spot, like extroversion. But curiosity or stress tolerance? Those stay hidden. Roles distort things too. You might act like a Club at work but feel like a Heart inside.

Here's the bottom line: How others see you shapes how they work with you.

If they only see part of you, the wrong part gets reinforced.

Comparing how you see yourself with how others see you reveals where those misalignments exist. The gaps show you what needs realigning.

The Gifting Ceremony

One of the most powerful ways to expose the gaps between self-perception and how others see us is through a "Gifting Ceremony." It's a simple yet profound exercise for small teams who know each other well.

With cards: Spread several decks face up on a table. Ask each person to pick a card that describes someone in the room.

Without cards: Ask each person to write down a trait or strength they see in each teammate.

Then the ceremony begins. One person stands, picks someone, and speaks directly to them, not the group.

They share a quick story of appreciation: "Remember that chaotic deadline? You broke everything down and helped us focus. That's why I am gifting you the 'organized' card."

The moment is personal, real, and often emotional.

Each person gets to give and receive feedback that feels genuine, not corporate. Sometimes people see themselves the same way others do. Sometimes they don't.

I once worked with a crew of construction workers. Big, burly, bearded guys. During the gifting ceremony, one worker gave another the "self-sacrificing" card.

The receiver's eyes teared up.

He'd always seen himself as a Club—just a guy who delivered results. But his coworker told the story of how he was always the one who fell on the sword when things went wrong. How he gave himself in a way no one else did.

He'd never seen it. But they had.

The room went quiet. These tough guys just witnessed someone being truly seen.

The Gifting Ceremony makes that gap visible. No surveys. No reports. Just a simple gesture—whether a physical card or spoken words—from someone who says, "This is how I experience you."

Sometimes that confirms what you know. Sometimes it reveals what you've been denying. And other times, it shows you something you never knew about yourself.

That's the gift of gifting. It shows you who you are and how others experience you. When those two don't match, it can lead to misunderstandings and missed opportunities.

PUT IT INTO PLAY

The gap between how you see yourself and how others see you reveals hidden opportunities. You don't need cards for any of these steps, just stories.

 **Ask three to five people for input.** Choose colleagues, friends, or team members who know you well. Ask them: "What's one trait you see in me that stands out?"

 **Compare their answers to your self-assessment.** Look at the suits you identified for yourself in Chapter 1. Do others see you the same way? Where do the views align? Where do they differ?

 **Don't dismiss the gaps.** If others consistently see something you don't, there's truth there. Either you're hiding your real self, or you've adapted to a role that doesn't fit.

 **Share what you discovered.** Tell your team or close colleagues: "Here's how I see myself, and here's how you see me. Let's talk about the gap." That conversation builds trust and clarity.

 **Adjust if needed.** If you're playing a suit that drains you (like Rick the city manager), delegate those tasks to someone whose natural strength it is.

Your self-perception and others' perception line up only 50 percent of the time. That's the gift of gifting—it reveals the gap between who you are and how others experience you.

Next Hand: *You've learned how to play your hand. Now it's time to play with others. Part Two is about teams, collaboration, culture, and innovation. You'll learn how to leverage individual strengths for collective wins.* →

PART TWO

PLAYING TO WIN TOGETHER

How to Build, Lead, and Win with a Full Deck

You've seen your own cards.

You know your strengths, your blind spots, and how others read your hand.

But the real game doesn't happen alone. It happens across the table.

This part is about what happens when your cards meet theirs—when personalities combine to create something new.

Here, we move from the individual to the collective. From self-awareness to shared awareness. From your hand to the whole table.

Part Two operates at the Team, Meetings, and Organization levels.

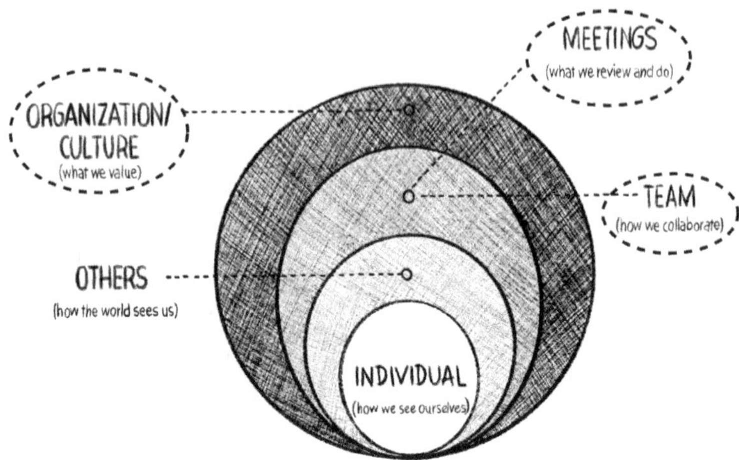

You'll learn how to:

- Better understand others on your team
- Lead your team with a full deck
- Balance and structure powerful meetings
- Build a culture that drives performance and retention
- Optimize the innovation process using all four suits
- Create environments where everyone can thrive
- Sell and market more effectively

When everyone plays to their strong suit, and you play with a full deck, the whole table wins.

CHAPTER 6

WINNING WITH A PAIR

Why Two Opposites Beat Ten Clones

~~~~~~

You can win big with only a pair if you play it right. The right duo can create balance and drive innovation.

~~~~~~

Think about history's great pairs: Jobs and Wozniak, Lennon and McCartney, Kirk and Spock.

Opposites who made each other better. Alone they were incomplete. Together they were unstoppable.

Most leaders do the opposite. They hire people like themselves. When everyone thinks alike, blind spots multiply.

A pair of **Diamonds** generates ideas but never finishes.
A pair of **Clubs** delivers on time but never stretches.
A pair of **Spades** gets lost in analysis.
A pair of **Hearts** keeps everyone happy but avoids hard truths.

But pairing opposites isn't easy. The differences that create balance also create tension. If you're not prepared for it, that tension can tear teams apart.

I once worked with a CEO who was a fiery Diamond. Her COO was a detail-driven Club who shut down half her ideas. To her, he was the "Department of No." To him, she was the "Queen of Chaos."

At first they struggled to work together. It felt counterproductive.

But once they understood their suits, the tension made sense. They didn't need less conflict. They needed *better* conflict.

Good Conflict and Bad Conflict

There are two types of conflict: task conflict and relationship conflict.

Task conflict is about ideas—it's healthy.
Relationship conflict is about people—it's toxic.

Teams that understand their styles don't avoid conflict. They work through it. Teams that ignore differences let emotions fester until people withdraw or explode.

Conflict is inevitable. You can design for it, or you can let it take control.

A study of medical teams in New Zealand found that different styles, when not structured properly, created chaos rather than the brilliance they should have unlocked.

Doctors, nurses, and specialists brought unique perspectives. That should have been the magic. Instead, they clashed.

Some shut down. Others got angry. Patient care suffered.

Different thinkers don't automatically work well together. They need structure, clarity, and appreciation. Without these, teams stay stuck or fall apart.

I saw this at a global oil and gas company. On paper, their team was balanced—a perfect mix of suits.

But the balance was an illusion.

Hearts were in HR.
Spades in R&D.
Clubs in operations.
Diamonds in marketing.

Each department was a perfect silo. Collaboration rarely happened.

Each group made smart local improvements, but no breakthroughs. Innovation stalled because no one was playing together.

The solution: bring the suits together intentionally, not accidentally.

Valuing All of the Suits

When I play Personality Poker with groups, we break into suits and answer four questions:

1. What's your suit's greatest contribution?
2. When do you feel underappreciated?
3. How do you drive others crazy?
4. Who drives you crazy, and why?

These questions spark laughter, honesty, and insight—especially number two. It surfaces the quiet resentment that comes from not feeling valued. This is the key to productive tension.

Jerry Hirshberg, former head of Nissan Design International, made it a practice to hire in pairs: free-form thinkers with methodical planners, analytical minds with dreamers.

The result wasn't harmony. It was constructive conflict that made solutions stronger.

That's the power of appreciation. It's not about avoiding differences. It's about designing for them.

Spades bring facts. Clubs bring order. Diamonds bring ideas. Hearts bring connection. You need all four at the table.

Innovation doesn't fail because people are different. It fails because they don't value those differences.

When people understand each other's styles, judgment fades. Appreciation drives collaboration.

PUT IT INTO PLAY

Opposites don't naturally attract, but they can create break-through results when you design for healthy tension.

 **Map your team's suits.** List everyone on your current project. Which suit is each person? Look for patterns. Are you all the same?

 **Pair opposites intentionally.** For your next initiative, deliberately partner a Spade with a Heart, or a Diamond with a Club. Give them a shared goal and watch what happens.

 **Name the conflict type.** When tension arises, ask: "Is this about the idea (task conflict) or about each other (relationship conflict)?" Task conflict is productive. Relationship conflict isn't.

 **Run the four questions.** If your team knows their suits, gather by suit and answer the questions from the chapter. Share responses in a safe environment.

 **Create a shared language.** When a Diamond and Club clash, reframe it: "She's not being reckless; she's exploring possibilities. He's not killing ideas; he's stress-testing them." When a Heart and Spade clash: "She's not avoiding the data; she's prioritizing people. He's not being cold; he's being objective." Appreciation makes pushback productive.

Innovation doesn't fail because people are different. It fails because they don't value those differences.

Next Hand: *You've seen how opposites can clash or create something extraordinary. Next, we'll split the deck by color: black and red, rational and relational.* →

CHAPTER 7

RATIONAL MINDS VS. RELATIONAL MINDS

Why You Need Both to Innovate

In Personality Poker, the colors reveal your thinking style, which is critical for collaboration and leadership.

The black cards—Clubs and Spades—are rational. They focus on stability and practicality.

The red cards—Hearts and Diamonds—are relational. They make connections between people and ideas.

Black cards put the "no" in inNOvation. They see the reasons something won't work, and frequently respond with "yeah, but."

Red cards put the fun in dysFUNctional. Their trap is losing focus and getting distracted by new opportunities.

When one dominates, results suffer.

I saw this at a division of a major publishing company. Sales were down. Morale was low. The parent company was ready to sell it off, which meant many would lose their jobs.

We ran a Personality Poker session with the leadership team.

Halfway through, I made a joke I've told a hundred times: "If the leader of your company is a red, your business might end up in the red."

Usually that gets a laugh. This time, no one smiled. Everyone turned to the two co-leaders, each holding five red cards.

In seconds, we figured out what was wrong.

The leaders were fun, charismatic, and full of ideas. But they couldn't prioritize, focus, or finish. The division wasn't broken. It was spinning.

We added a new leader to the team who had five black cards.

She brought structure, set deadlines, and kept the team accountable. We provided training to help them work together effectively.

Within six months, the division delivered more innovation than in the previous eighteen.

The lesson was clear: When you have all one color, you either stall or spin out.

So what's really going on? It comes down to how we think. Some people go deep, others make connections.

Rational vs. Relational Thinking

Dot Thinking vs. Line Thinking

I once worked with two colleagues, Lisa and Brad.

Lisa was analytical and methodical. Brad was wildly creative and had a gift for reading people.

When Lisa learned something new, her first question was, "What does this mean?" I call this **dot thinking**—going deep and finding logic.

Brad's first question was, "What is this like?" That's **line thinking**—connecting dots and seeing patterns.

The card colors reflect this distinction.

Black cards are dot thinkers. They go deep so ideas stay grounded.

Sun Tzu described them well: "Strategy without tactics is the slowest route to victory. Tactics without strategy is the noise before defeat."

Black cards analyze what matters, then execute to make it real.

Red cards are line thinkers. They connect dots—linking experiences, ideas, and people to drive creativity.

Steve Jobs captured this perfectly: "Creativity is just connecting things." The most creative people have "had more experiences" and can "connect experiences they've had and synthesize new things."

Red cards see connections across experiences and people, turning them into something new.

Both are essential. Black cards bring depth and practicality. Red cards bring creativity and relationships.

But they often misunderstand each other.

To red cards, black cards can seem like idea killers. But they're not stopping innovation—they're safeguarding it.

To black cards, red cards look impulsive, chasing shiny ideas. But they're not careless—they're exploring what others can't yet see.

The secret isn't to silence one color but to play both at once.

If your team is full of red cards, who's turning vision into reality? If it's all black cards, who's building relationships and challenging the status quo?

Balance the colors, and you balance the business.

PUT IT INTO PLAY

Black cards go deep on the details. Red cards connect ideas and people. You need both to innovate.

 **Check your team's color balance.** Look at your leadership team or project group. Count the red cards (creative, relational, idea-driven) versus the black cards (practical, analytical, structured). All one color? That's your problem.

 **Pair opposites on key decisions.** Before launching something new, put a red card and black card in the room together. Let the red card explore possibilities. Let the black card stress-test them.

 **Reframe resistance as insight.** When a black card says no, ask: "What risk are you protecting us from?" When a red card pitches ten ideas, ask: "Which one excites you most and why?" Then ask together: "How can we move forward while addressing the risk?" or "How can we test this without losing focus?"

 **Know your own thinking style.** When you learn something new, do you ask "What does this mean?" (dot thinking/black) or "What is this like?" (line thinking/red)? Recognize your default so you can seek the opposite perspective.

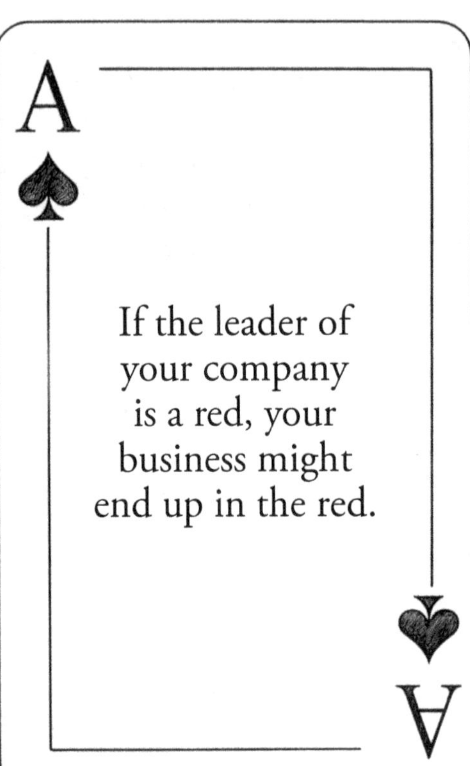

Next Hand: *Knowing the colors is only part of the equation. The next chapter explores the real structure behind team-work: rules matter more than roles.* →

CHAPTER 8

WHY RULES MATTER MORE THAN THE ROLES

People Thrive in the Right Environment, Regardless of the Task

Matching the task to the suit isn't the biggest factor in performance. It's putting people in the right environment that matches their style.

Most leaders focus on matching people to tasks. Designers design. Builders build. Red cards create. Black cards execute.

But that simple logic misses the real driver of performance.

It's not the task that matters. It's the environment.

Unfortunately, when employees struggle, leaders try to fix the person, not the environment.

A leadership course at Eckerd College in Florida proved this in an unexpected way.

Several years ago, managers in the program were tested to determine their style—their color in Personality Poker.

Red cards thrive on doing things differently and breaking rules.

Black cards excel at doing things better with structure and following rules.

The managers were then split into teams for a problem-solving exercise.

Each team had two groups. The "designers" would create the solution, and a separate group of "builders" would implement it.

There were three setups:

- **Team One** used red cards as designers and black cards as builders.
- **Team Two** mixed both styles together in both roles.
- **Team Three** flipped it around, with the black cards doing the design and the red cards responsible for the build.

In addition, the design task was highly structured, with seven rules that had to be followed. The build task had almost no rules.

Which team do you think was most effective?

When I ask audiences this question, no one picks Team One.

Ironically, that's how most organizations build teams.

They put the creative people (the red cards) on the design side and hand everything off to the black-card implementers.

Most people pick Team Two. It *should* work. It's the "full deck" approach, right?

But Team Two was the least effective.

They didn't have the tools to communicate or collaborate. Every time a red card shared an idea, a black card shut it down. Communication collapsed.

Surprisingly, Team Three won by a mile.

Why?

The **black cards worked best in the structured design role**.

The **red cards thrived in the flexible build role without any rules**.

The lesson? When people are matched to the right environment, they excel. When they're dropped into the wrong one, they flounder.

Environment Matters More Than Tasks

Red cards prefer environments with little structure. They enjoy shaping the unknown and defining the undefined.

Black cards perform best when the rules are clear. They thrive in structured environments with clear expectations.

Get this wrong, and you frustrate everyone.

Put a red card in a rule-bound process and they suffocate. Put a black card in a wide-open space and they freeze.

Get it right, and the magic happens.

Red cards can implement brilliantly when the environment is

fluid. Black cards can ideate effectively when the environment has structure.

The study proved what leaders often miss: it's not about the task, it's about the conditions. I learned this the hard way in my own business.

I had a complex client engagement with multiple workstreams and brought on Sean, a black card with deep project management experience, to run it. I stepped back and let him work his magic.

That's my red card style. I trust people. I give them space. I let them figure it out. It works for me, so I unconsciously assumed it would work for everyone.

Three weeks later, Sean was struggling. Deliverables were late. The work was surprisingly disorganized. I was frustrated. He seemed capable, so why wasn't he executing?

When I finally asked, he was direct: "You haven't given me enough direction. I don't know what 'good' looks like. What are the milestones? The decision framework? How do you want me to structure the workstreams?"

He was right. I'd given him a black card task but created a red card environment—minimal structure, figure-it-out-as-you-go. I thought I was empowering him, but I was starving him.

The moment I gave Sean clear rules and defined milestones with explicit success criteria, he took off. Same person. Same role. Different rules.

I didn't fail to match him to the right work. I failed to give him the right environment to do that work well.

So don't just deal out tasks. Deal out the work with the rules in mind. That's how you get the right people in the right roles at the right time.

PUT IT INTO PLAY

Matching people to the right environment matters more than matching them to the right task.

 **Audit your next three assignments.** For each one, ask: "What are the rules here?" Is it highly structured (clear process, defined steps) or wide open (ambiguous, exploratory)?

 **Match people to the environment, not just the task.** Give structured tasks to black cards and open-ended tasks to red cards.

 **Break the creative/execution stereotype.** Don't automatically assume red = creative work and black = execution. A black card can design brilliantly in a structured environment. A red card can build effectively in a flexible one.

 **Test it with one project.** Pick an upcoming initiative. Identify whether it's rule-heavy or rule-light. Then assign people based on environment fit, not task stereotype. Track the results.

 **When people struggle, check the rules.** If someone's disengaged or underperforming, ask: "Are they in the wrong environment?"

When people are
matched in the
right environment,
they excel. When
they're dropped
in the wrong one,
they flounder. It's
not about the task.
It's about the rules
that govern it.

Next Hand: *Rules create clarity, but success comes from execution. Next, we'll see how to deal out responsibilities so every suit contributes where they're strongest.* →

CHAPTER 9

DEALING OUT THE HAND

How to Make Teams More Balanced and Effective

We prefer working with people who are similar to us. This isn't always bad—it depends on the hand you're playing. Sometimes sameness is efficient. Other times, it means you're fast at being wrong.

A study led by Clint Bowers at the University of Central Florida examined 500 teams across thirteen studies to answer one question: How does personality diversity really affect performance?

At first glance, the results looked flat. Diverse teams didn't outperform same-style teams. But that wasn't the full story.

When researchers dug deeper, the type of task made all the difference.

For simple, routine work, what they called "low difficulty" tasks, teams that thought alike actually performed better. Too much diversity slowed them down. Everyone pulled in different directions, but the work didn't need that.

However, for complex, uncertain work, the full deck came alive. Diverse teams consistently outperformed the rest.

Leadership and Innovation Require Diversity

For high-stakes work like innovation, you need multiple perspectives and some creative conflict.

At the Wharton School, researchers studied top management teams at major corporations. Their finding was clear: diversity at the top drives profit at the bottom.

Companies whose leadership teams mixed functions—finance, marketing, operations, human resources—delivered higher returns. The more perspectives at the table, the stronger the results.

In other words, playing with a full deck doesn't just spark innovation; it boosts financial performance.

So, when does sameness work and when does difference win?

For simple, repeatable work, sameness brings speed. For complex, creative work, diversity drives results. The trick is knowing when to mix your cards and when to play one suit strong.

Once you've built the mix, the real game begins—how you deal the hand.

Diversity on paper doesn't create innovation. It's what you do with it that counts. The best teams don't just collect different suits; they play them strategically.

Busting Silos

One operations team in the energy industry wanted to improve efficiency, but they struggled.

They were doing all the right things, yet nothing was moving forward. The project scope kept growing. The goals kept shifting. Uneasiness grew.

They needed a way to bring everyone's perspective in earlier, stay aligned on what "done" meant, and use their differences as advantages.

That's where Personality Poker came in.

Instead of treating projects like marathons, they treated each one like a sprint. Each project was a new hand.

Each suit did what it did best. Spades brought data. Diamonds generated ideas. Clubs built the plan. Hearts kept people aligned. Everyone had a role.

But surprisingly, the real value came when they temporarily *shifted* the roles.

Spades worried about people.
Diamonds focused on plans.
Hearts analyzed data.
Clubs imagined the future.

That shift changed everything. They built empathy for each other's styles and discovered new strengths.

Project drift stopped. Rework dropped. Accountability rose. Although the tension didn't disappear, it became productive.

Everyone still spent most of their time playing to their strong suit. But by shuffling the deck from time to time, it kept people fresh and appreciative.

Whether you're running a product launch, a marketing campaign, or a strategy off-site, the same principle applies.

Identify strong suits.
Balance the deck.
Rotate roles.
Deal out the work.

Divergent perspectives without design is chaos. With structure, appreciation, and empathy, it becomes innovation.

PUT IT INTO PLAY

Sameness works for simple tasks. Diversity wins for complex ones. Know which game you're playing.

 **Assess your current work.** Look at your team's projects. Are they routine and predictable, or complex and uncertain? Simple work rewards sameness. Complex work demands divergent perspectives.

 **Map the suits at your next kickoff.** Before starting a new project, identify which suit each team member is. Write it down. Do you have all four represented?

 **Assign roles by suit—at first.** Let Spades handle data and analysis. Diamonds generate ideas. Clubs build the plan. Hearts keep people aligned. Give everyone their natural role to start.

 **Shuffle halfway through.** Midway through the project, rotate roles. Have Spades focus on people. Let Diamonds worry about the plan. Ask Hearts to analyze data. Let Clubs imagine possibilities. This builds empathy and reveals hidden strengths.

For simple work, teams that think alike perform better. Too much diversity slows them down. However, for complex and uncertain work, the full deck comes alive.

Next Hand: *The way you deal the hand shapes how your team performs. Up next: how meetings have personalities—and how to design them to bring out every suit.* →

CHAPTER 10

MEETINGS HAVE PERSONALITIES TOO

Why Matching People to Meeting Styles Unlocks Better Results

Most people hate meetings. But it's not always the meetings themselves. Often, the meeting's personality clashes with the people in the room, or there are simply too many of the same kind.

After my first public session of Personality Poker twenty years ago, a CEO in the audience bought a stack of decks.

He first used them to assess people's personalities. Then he realized they worked even better for assessing the personalities of his meetings. And he discovered his meetings weren't always playing with a full deck.

Some meetings are **Spade meetings**. Data-heavy. Packed with charts, evidence, and analysis. Great for fact-driven thinkers. Torture for people who want action or energy.

Others are **Diamond meetings**. Big on brainstorming. Lots of "what if" and "wouldn't it be cool if." Perfect for innovators. Maddening for those who just want to know the plan.

Club meetings? Those are your status updates: timelines, deadlines, budgets. They bring order, but they drain people who thrive on ideas or relationships.

And then there are **Heart meetings**. Team-building. Recognition. Check-ins. They energize people but leave some wondering when the "real work" starts.

The CEO discovered that 90 percent of his meetings were Club meetings: status reports and project check-ins. There was little space for Spade analysis, Diamond ideas, or Heart connection.

No wonder his team struggled to innovate or stay energized. Their meeting mix was starving them.

His first move? Balance the deck.

Design Meetings That Play to Every Suit

He started naming the personality of each meeting. Then he cut back the Club meetings to make room for the others.

Next, he matched the meeting to the leader.

A Spade ran the data review.

A Diamond ran the brainstorm.

A Club ran the status check.

A Heart ran the team-building.

But he didn't stop there.

Before each meeting, he asked the leader to invite other suits to help shape the structure. That created an environment where every style could thrive.

Like Chapter 8 showed, rules matter more than roles. The same applies to meetings.

For example, a Club might work with a Diamond to make status updates more engaging by using short videos before the meeting instead of long monologues.

Or a Diamond might partner with a Club to add structure to brainstorming sessions so the black cards feel more at home.

Over time, the team built muscle. People learned to flex across styles. A Spade could run a Heart-style check-in. A Diamond could manage a Club-style timeline.

But early on, the CEO let people lead from their strengths while borrowing from others to cover the gaps.

The bottom line?

Meetings have personalities too. When you name them, balance them, align leaders with them, and design for all suits, meetings stop being a drain and start becoming a driver.

PUT IT INTO PLAY

Meetings have personalities. When you balance them, people stop dreading them and start contributing.

 **Audit your meetings for the next month.** List every recurring meeting and label its suit.

 **Count the imbalance.** Which suit dominates? If 80 percent are one type (usually Club status meetings), that's why people are disengaged.

 **Add what's missing.** All Club meetings? Schedule one Diamond brainstorm and one Heart check-in. All ideas, no execution? Add a Club accountability session.

 **Match leaders to meeting types.** Spades run data reviews. Diamonds lead brainstorms. Clubs run status updates. Hearts facilitate team-building. People lead best from their natural suit.

 **Design with opposites.** Before each meeting, have the leader invite someone from a different suit to help structure it. A Club helps a Diamond add focus. A Diamond helps a Club add creativity. This makes every style feel welcome.

Meetings have personalities too. When you name them, balance them, align leaders with them, and design for all suits, meetings stop being a drain and start becoming a driver.

Next Hand: *Meetings reflect personality, but culture magnifies it. Next, you'll see how great cultures celebrate differences and what happens when one suit dominates.* →

CHAPTER 11

Culture Starts with Cult

Why the Best Cultures Keep a Full Deck

Every company talks about culture as if it's an asset. But culture, left unchecked, can become a cult. Sameness gets rewarded. Difference gets discouraged. And innovation quietly dies.

I once worked with a logistics company that wanted to reinvent itself. We gathered the top twelve executives and played Personality Poker.

Each person picked two cards. One for what the company was good at and rewarded. One for what it needed but didn't have.

Almost everyone chose Clubs for the first card. Execution machines. Process-driven and disciplined.

And for the second? Nearly all picked Diamonds, especially the "experimental" card. That was the wake-up call.

The culture excelled at execution and dealing with complexity. But it struggled with experimentation and ambiguity. Once they saw it, they could change it.

A strong culture can be an asset. It creates belonging and stability. But the word "culture" literally starts with "cult."

And when everyone thinks alike, acts alike, and rewards alike, you're closer to running a cult than a culture.

Cults feel powerful. They create loyalty and identity. But they shut the door on difference, and that's when innovation fades.

When Culture Becomes a Clone Factory

This isn't about personality; it's about collective behavior. Over time, organizations hire, promote, and reward people who think the same and work the same.

I saw it at a Fortune 100 technology company. The longtime CEO loved data. When he played Personality Poker, he drew almost all Spades.

His leadership team looked the same. The company became Spade-heavy. Every decision required endless analysis.

It worked for a while. Then it didn't.

They couldn't see the forest for the spreadsheets. Hearts felt ignored and left. Creativity dried up. Progress stalled.

Research backs this up. Psychologists M. J. Kirton and R.

M. McCarthy found that every organization has a "cognitive climate," a collective personality.

When minority styles are ignored, they leave. What's left is comfort without creativity and stability without progress.

The same thing happens inside teams. When everyone thinks alike, minority voices go silent. Resentment grows. People disappear.

But cultures can be reshaped.

At a global design firm, the deck was all Diamonds. Ideas everywhere, but nothing shipped. They deliberately hired more Clubs: people who loved structure and deadlines.

Within a year, delivery doubled.

Balance matters.

The goal isn't to weaken your culture. It's to widen it.

Great cultures don't just celebrate alignment. They make space for difference.

They know that every strength, when overused, becomes a weakness.

When you bring in all four suits and value what each contributes, you get breakthrough results. People do their best work. Retention rises because everyone feels seen.

The best cultures aren't cults. They're collaborative.

PUT IT INTO PLAY

Your culture has a personality. If it's too narrow, innovation dies. Widen it intentionally.

 **Name what gets rewarded.** Ask your team: "What behaviors get promoted, praised, or prioritized here?" Write down the answers. Which suit dominates? (Execution = Clubs. Data = Spades. Ideas = Diamonds. People = Hearts.)

 **Name what's missing.** Now ask: "What should be rewarded but isn't?" The gap between these two answers reveals your cultural blind spot.

 **Do the two-card exercise.** Gather your leadership team. Have each person pick two cards (or traits): one for what the company rewards, one for what it needs but lacks. Look for patterns. That's your wake-up call. No cards? Just use words that describe the culture.

 **Hire for the gap.** If one or two suits dominate your culture, deliberately hire for the missing suits. Don't hire for fit; hire to complete the deck.

 **Publicly celebrate all suits.** In team meetings, recognition emails, or performance reviews, explicitly call out contributions from every style. Match the feedback to the suit.

The goal isn't to weaken your culture. It's to widen it. Great cultures don't just celebrate alignment. They make space for difference. Don't hire for fit; hire to complete the deck.

Next Hand: *A strong culture sets the stage for innovation. The next chapter reveals how each suit drives a different part of the innovation process, and what happens when one is missing.* →

CHAPTER 12

Innovation Isn't Just About Ideas

Why Every Suit Matters in the Innovation Process

Most people think innovation starts with an idea. It doesn't. It starts with a problem or opportunity worth solving. Jumping straight to ideas without a problem is like bringing a ladder before you know what you're climbing.

A global hospitality company had no shortage of ideas. Brainstorms, whiteboards, sticky notes. Red cards everywhere.

But growth had stalled.

They were missing the Spades who ask, "What problem are we solving?"

The company chased trends, launched new products, and burned money. Creativity wasn't the issue. Focus was.

A manufacturing client had the opposite problem. They were packed with Spades and Clubs, people obsessed with data and discipline.

They defined problems well and built solid plans but lacked Diamonds. They solved everything with the same old methods. Incremental improvements. No breakthroughs.

My $30 million Accenture project team struggled in a similar way. We had Diamonds and Hearts, a few Spades, but no Clubs. Great at ideas. Terrible at implementation.

Different companies, same root cause: missing suits.

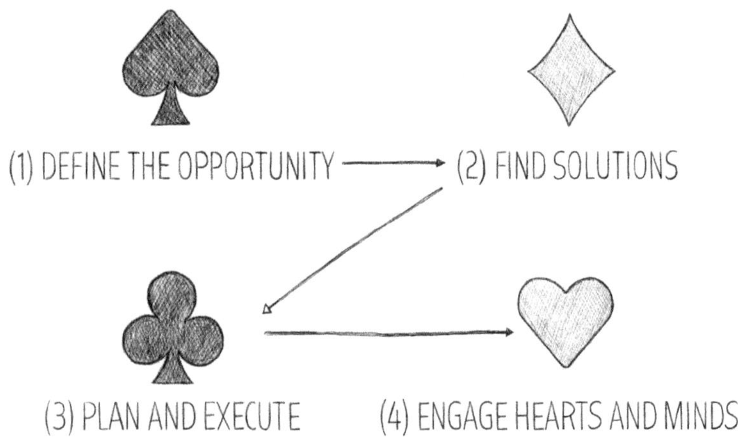

The Suits and the Innovation Process

The Innovation Rhythm

Innovation isn't a straight line. It loops, tests, and adapts. It's not as linear as I show it here, but the sequence still matters.

Each suit brings a rhythm. Together, they move ideas through solutions to results.

1. Define the Challenge (Spades).

Most innovation efforts fail because they start with ideas instead of insights. The best teams begin by framing the problem or opportunity.

What's broken, what needs fixing, and what's worth pursuing?

Spades ask better questions. Their data and analysis expose what's needed rather than what's new.

Innovation isn't just creative. It's analytical.

2. Generate Solutions (Diamonds).

Once you know the right problem or opportunity, it's time to think creatively.

What can you borrow from another industry or experience? How can you challenge assumptions and uncover new angles?

Diamonds connect ideas others overlook. They link patterns across unrelated fields and imagine what doesn't yet exist.

They generate possibilities from insights.

3. Plan and Execute (Clubs).

Ideas without execution don't create value. This is where Clubs shine.

They plan the work and work the plan. They bring discipline, structure, and accountability. They create movement and deliver results.

But innovation isn't linear. It's iterative.

The best innovators run small, fast experiments: build it, test it, fix it, then learn, adjust, and repeat.

That's where experimentation meets execution. Diamonds excel at testing and exploring. Clubs excel at implementing and scaling. Both are essential. Together, they create a powerful innovation engine.

4. Engage the Hearts and Minds (Hearts).

Throughout the process, you need the Hearts. They bring people along. They rally teams around ideas, build trust across functions, and make sure solutions meet real human needs.

Innovation doesn't happen in a vacuum. It happens *through* people and it is *for* people. Hearts create buy-in. They make people feel invested, not just informed. That's what overcomes resistance and builds momentum.

The best ideas die without adoption. Hearts bridge the gap between what's possible and what people will actually embrace. They listen, connect, and build the momentum that makes change stick.

Follow the rhythm, and ideas move from insight to impact. Skip a step, and you end up in analysis, chaos, or politics.

A Full Deck Still Needs a Dealer

At one corporate retreat, twenty-four leaders were split into four teams of six people. Two teams had a balanced mix of suits. The other two were lopsided.

Each team was challenged to make a short "movie" overnight about how to grow their business. They had complete freedom to do what they wanted, as long as their video was two to three minutes long.

Who won?

The all-Diamond team brainstormed in the bar but didn't finish filming. Although they had fantastic ideas, in the end, they had nothing to show…other than a hangover.

The team with only Clubs and Spades delivered a polished yet unexciting video. While creating it, they seemed bored and disengaged. They lacked the Diamonds and Hearts who would bring ideas and people to life.

One team had all four suits yet still failed miserably. The problem? Everyone insisted on doing everything. They argued through the night. It was chaos. Their mediocre video did worse than the Club/Spade team.

The winning team also had all four suits, but they dealt out the work. Spades defined the concept. Diamonds wrote the story. Clubs kept everyone on track. Hearts kept morale high and injected humor.

The lesson: Creativity without structure isn't innovation. You need all the suits, *and* you need to assign clear roles.

Missing Suits = Poor Innovation

Personality Poker was first developed not as a personality test, but as an innovation diagnostic. It helps identify why innovation is failing by revealing which suits are missing.

No Spades? No focus.

No Diamonds? No breakthroughs.

No Clubs? No delivery.

No Hearts? No buy-in.

Innovation isn't about having the best ideas. It's about having all the perspectives you need to make ideas real.

PUT IT INTO PLAY

Innovation breaks when suits are missing. Before you launch anything, make sure all four are in the room.

 **Map your innovation process.** Write down the stages of your next initiative and label each by suit: Define the Challenge (Spade), Generate Solutions (Diamond), Plan and Execute (Club), Engage the Hearts and Minds (Heart).

 **Identify the gap.** Which suit is missing or underrepresented? That's where your innovation will break down.

 **Ask these four questions throughout.** (1) What problem are we solving? (Spades) (2) What possibilities haven't we considered? (Diamonds) (3) Who's making it happen and how? (Clubs) (4) Who's coming with us? (Hearts)

 **Assign roles by suit.** Spades define and validate. Diamonds generate options. Clubs build the plan and track progress. Hearts keep people aligned. Don't let everyone do everything.

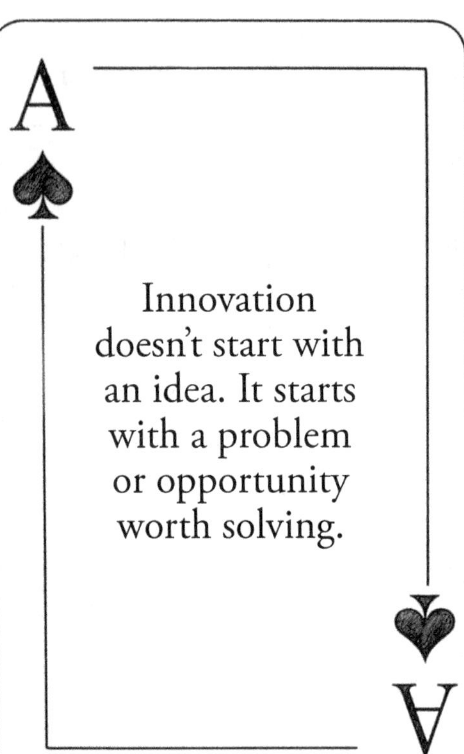

Next Hand: *Innovation generates ideas. Selling turns them into action. Up next: how to communicate with every suit using logic, emotion, structure, and vision so people say yes.* → 

CHAPTER 13

SELLING WITH A FULL DECK

How the Cards Can Help You Close More Deals

Every conversation is a sale. You might be selling a product, an idea, or a change. Whether you're talking to a customer, a team, or an audience, you're always selling something.

Selling isn't manipulation. It's alignment. It's about helping others see value in what you see.

But here's the catch. Most people sell the way *they* want to buy.

A Spade uses facts.

A Heart tells stories.

A Club gives steps.

A Diamond paints dreams.

Each approach works only for people who think the same way.

Selling in your own style is like speaking your native language and assuming everyone else speaks it. That's why you need to know your customer's suit.

If you communicate the wrong way, your message falls flat. It's not that they disagreed. They just didn't feel understood. That's why you need to sell with a full deck.

The Power of a Full Deck Pitch Deck

A CEO once told me how Personality Poker saved a critical board presentation.

She led a mid-sized tech company and was a strong Diamond. Her team's pitch to the board reflected her style: bold ideas, big vision.

Fifteen minutes in, she looked around the room. Silence. Folded arms. Eyes down. They were losing the room.

Then she remembered: her board was full of Spades and Clubs. They didn't want excitement. They wanted evidence and a plan.

So she stopped mid-presentation. "Let's look at the real problem we're solving," she said, "and what it's costing us." Then she showed data and laid out the plan.

The shift was instant. The room leaned in.

Once the Spades had their proof and the Clubs had their actions, the ideas landed.

They didn't change the message. They changed the order. And that changed everything.

The Framework Behind Every Great Message

Long before marketing funnels and sales scripts, Aristotle figured out how persuasion really works.

He said every great message comes down to three things: credibility (ethos), emotion (pathos), and logic (logos). Today, we often add a fourth: purpose (telos), the "why" that gives meaning to it all.

1. Start with Credibility (Spades).

Aristotle said persuasion begins with *ethos*: credibility. People must believe you before they'll believe your idea.

The listener is asking, "Why should I listen to you?" and "Do you actually understand what's going on?"

Credibility is earned not through credentials but through clarity.

The listener must believe you know their problem in a way that feels sharper and truer than how they would describe it themselves.

A reframing, a counterintuitive insight, or a precise diagnosis establishes authority instantly.

This speaks powerfully to the Spades in the room.

2. Move to Emotion (Hearts).

Once they know you understand the problem, they need to know you understand *them* and their pain. That's *pathos*: the emotional core of persuasion.

Hearts tune into emotion. They ask, "Do you really get what this feels like?"

This isn't about sympathy. It's about recognition. Surface the internal struggle people rarely articulate out loud. Put words to the frustration, fear, or aspiration they recognize immediately.

Say, "You've been working late nights and still can't close the gap." That's the shared pain that builds trust.

When people feel understood, they trust you to guide them. And only then are they ready for your plan.

3. Add Logic (Clubs).

The first two steps tee up the problem and the pain. Now you can move to *logos:* logic and structure.

Only now does the listener ask, "What's the solution?" or "How does this work?"

Clubs want the answer and a clear plan.

Outline the path forward in plain language. Three steps. Two milestones. One clear goal. This might include specific calls to action you want from them.

This calms anxiety by turning ideas into solutions and actions. Skip this, and your pitch feels like a wish.

At this point, add data to further satisfy the Spades.

4. End with Vision (Diamonds).

Finally, bring it home with imagination. Diamonds want to dream. They ask, "What could this become?"

This is your *telos*: the higher purpose, the transformation. Paint a picture they can feel.

"Imagine a team that finishes strong every time. Imagine customers who love working with us."

Logic tells you what to do. Vision makes you want to do it.

People don't buy because they're convinced. They buy because they feel understood. That's the power of a full-deck pitch.

PUT IT INTO PLAY

Everyone sells. To be as effective as possible, you need all four suits. Balance them, and people don't just listen. They buy in.

 **Map your next conversation using the four suits.** Outline your message in four parts: 1) Problem/credibility (Spade), 2) Emotional connection (Heart), 3) Clear solution/plan (Club), 4) Inspiring vision (Diamond).

 **Start with the problem, not the solution.** Lead with a story that shows you understand what's broken. Spades need to trust you before they'll listen.

 **Name the feeling.** After establishing the problem, connect emotionally. What's the frustration? The fear? The cost of inaction? Hearts need to feel understood before they'll follow.

 **Give them a solution and a clear path.** Outline a few concrete steps. Clubs need structure. Without it, your pitch feels unachievable.

 **End with possibility.** Paint a picture of what success looks like. Diamonds need to dream before they'll commit.

 **Read the room and reorder if needed.** If you're losing your audience, pause and switch to a different suit.

 **Match the style in one-on-one conversations.** When talking with an individual, connection matters more than sequence. Spot their suit (review Chapter 4), then meet them where they are.

Every conversation is a sale. It's about helping others see value in what you see. But here's the catch: most people sell the way they want to buy—and that only works for people who think like them.

Next Hand: *Now that you've learned to play well with others, it's time to master your own game. Part Three digs deeper into how you grow, adapt, and play to your full potential.* →

PART THREE
MASTERING YOUR HAND

Going Deeper into the Inner Game

You've learned your suit. You've played with others. Now it's time to master your own game.

Self-awareness is the first step. Mastery comes when you use that awareness with intention. Great players know when to play their suit strong and when to adapt.

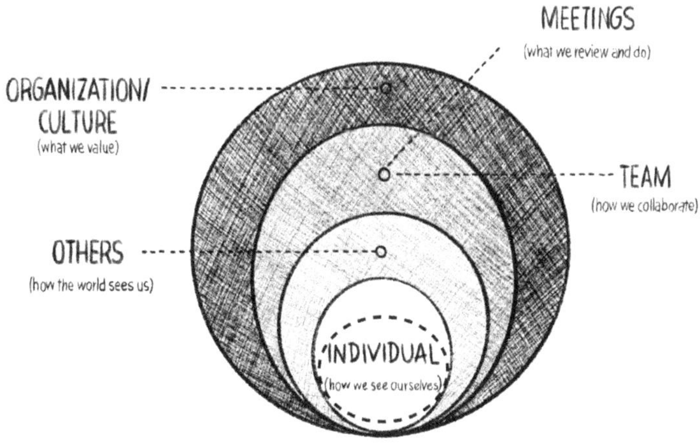

We're back at the Individual level, but this time, we're going deeper.

In this part, you'll learn how to:

- Double down on your strong suits without overplaying them
- Understand how your energy style shapes the way you play
- Recognize when your strong suit has gone too far
- Leverage the unique edge that comes from combining two suits
- Get to the "real" you at a deeper level

The goal isn't to put you in a box. It's about giving you clarity.

Mastery isn't about the cards you were dealt. It's how you play them.

CHAPTER 14

SHOWING YOUR TRUE HAND

Why Hiding Your Strong Suit Hurts You and Your Team

You've got a style that comes naturally. But are you using it intentionally? Sometimes we hide our strong suits. And we pay the price.

I was hired to run a Personality Poker session for an advertising agency.

Before we started, one of the employees, Sally, pulled me aside. "After today's event, I'm giving my two weeks' notice. I'm just not happy here."

I told her I understood and encouraged her to play full out anyway.

When we played Personality Poker, Sally chose all Diamonds. She saw herself as creative and imaginative.

But when her colleagues dealt her cards, every one of them gave her Spades.

Why? She was known as the master of spreadsheets. She was great at them, so people kept giving her more.

The problem? She hated spreadsheets. That work drained her. Yet she never said a word. She didn't want to be labeled a complainer, so she suffered in silence.

It didn't take long to see what was wrong. I met with the CEO and suggested a simple change: move Sally to the creative team and hire someone else to handle the data work.

Once she returned to what she loved—brainstorming, designing, and pitching ideas—everything changed. She was happier, more productive, and far more valuable to the company.

That's the power of showing your true hand. When you show people who you really are and play the hand that fits you best, everyone wins.

Why We Don't Show Our True Hand

Skills tell you what you *can* do. Your strong suit tells you what you *should* do.

It's not just what you're good at. It's what gives you energy.

But we often hide who we really are. We portray ourselves the way we think the world will approve. We hide our true hand because we fear judgment, rejection, or being seen as difficult.

Sally wore the Spade mask because she was good at it and people needed it. But it robbed her—and her team—of what she really brought to the table.

When you hide your strong suit, work feels like a grind. When you play to it, work feels like play. That's not just good for you. It's great for business.

Show Your True Hand

The secret is to stop fighting your strong suit and start owning it.

This doesn't mean ignoring the other suits. Awareness of your style and the styles of others makes you a stronger team player. But it does mean being honest about what energizes you and what drains you.

Be true to yourself. Be the best version of you. And allow others to do the same.

When you do, you don't just perform better. You enjoy the process more because you're playing the game you were built to win.

Stop hiding the real you. Show your true hand. Give the world your gifts.

PUT IT INTO PLAY

Your strong suit is your superpower. Stop hiding it. Start using it intentionally.

 **Identify the cards you're hiding.** What role are you playing that doesn't feel like you? Are you acting like a Spade when you're really a Diamond? A Club when you're a Heart? Write them down.

 **Name what energizes versus what drains you.** List one activity that gives you energy and one that exhausts you (even if you're good at it). The gap between them reveals which cards you're hiding.

 **Ask: "What am I hiding?"** Like Sally, are people giving you work based on what you *can* do instead of what you *should* do? If yes, you're wearing the wrong suit.

 **Have the conversation.** Tell your manager or team: "I've been playing [role], but my strong suit is [X]. Can we redistribute the work so I do more of what I'm built for?"

 **Show one card this week.** Pick one task you force yourself to do that drains you. Find someone whose strong suit matches that task, then delegate or trade it. Let them see your true hand.

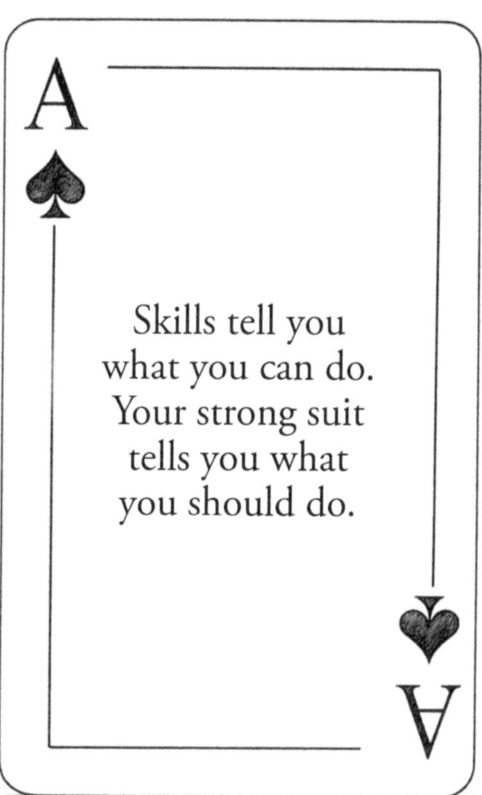

Next Hand: Once you've claimed your strong suit, it's time to understand how it shows up. The next chapter explores the numbers: your natural rhythm and pace. → 

CHAPTER 15

INWARD VS. OUTWARD ENERGY

How Two People with the Same Suit
Can Seem Completely Different

Not everyone with the same suit acts alike. In addition to the suits and colors, the numbers on your cards also have meaning. They reveal your energy style—how you express your suit in the world.

<hr>

When playing Personality Poker, both Mark and Sue turned out to be Hearts. Yet they couldn't have been more different.

Mark was outgoing and animated. He knew everyone, and everyone knew him.

Sue was quiet and reflective. She didn't have a large circle of friends, but her connections ran deep.

Same suit. Different volume.

The difference was in the numbers on their cards.

In this chapter, we'll look at the card numbers found in a standard deck. The 2, 3, and 4 cards are unique and are discussed in the next chapter.

In this chapter, we explore the cards 5 through Ace. These reveal whether your energy is directed inward or outward. That difference shapes how you think, lead, and show up in the world.

Energy Level Overview

Inwardly focused players

These individuals are represented by the 5 through 9 cards (5, 6, 7, 8, and 9).

They prefer depth over breadth. Reflection over reaction.

They thrive in smaller groups or solo work and are thoughtful and reliable.

Inwardly focused individuals are not necessarily shy or introverted. They aren't hiding. They simply prefer a quieter pace.

Outwardly focused players

These individuals are the 10 through Ace cards (10, Jack, Queen, King, and Ace).

They feed off energy. They thrive in groups.

They crave action, stimulation, and momentum.

When nothing is happening, they lose steam, so they stir things up.

The Energy Levels for Each Suit

Both energy levels matter. Although the differences appear in every suit, they are more pronounced with the Hearts and Clubs.

An **inward Spade** dives deep into analysis. Quiet researcher. Careful problem solver.
An **outward Spade** debates, defends data, and drives decisions with logic.

An **inward Diamond** sketches ideas in solitude. Perfects concepts quietly.
An **outward Diamond** pitches ideas with passion. Energizes a room with creativity.

An **inward Club** builds systems methodically. They like process and planning.
An **outward Club** is less concerned with how the work gets done; they just want to make sure it gets done. They are focused on actions and results.

An **inward Heart** listens deeply. Builds strong one-on-one bonds. They value the depth of their relationships.
An **outward Heart** is the social butterfly. They're great talkers. They know everyone.

The number adds nuance. It explains why two people in the same suit can feel so different.

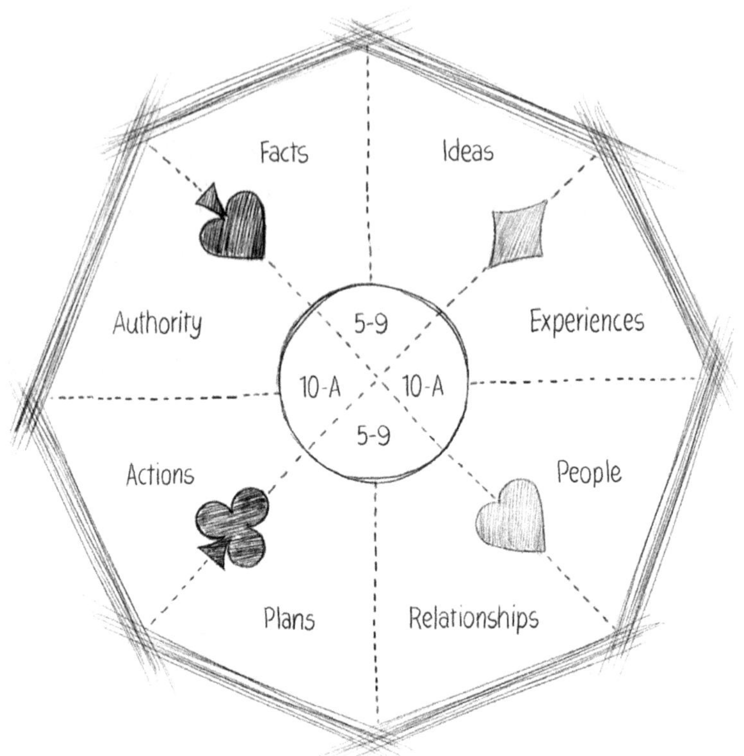

The Impact of the Number—Energy

This is why Mark, with his 10–Ace of Hearts hand, felt so different from Sue, who held mainly 5–9 of Hearts. He was talkative, and she was a great listener.

When you look at your hand, don't just notice the suit; look at the number. It shows whether your energy flows inward or outward and how that flow shapes the game you play.

PUT IT INTO PLAY

Your energy style—inward or outward—shapes how you show up. Know it, own it, and partner with the opposite. You don't need the cards to see where you land.

 **Identify your energy direction.** Do you prefer deep one-on-one conversations or energizing group settings? Quiet reflection or active brainstorming? That reveals whether you're inward (5–9) or outward (10–Ace).

 **Look at your cards (if you've played).** Are your top cards mostly 5–9 (inward) or 10–Ace (outward)? Write it down.

 **Name one strength, one limitation.** How does your energy style help you? ("I build deep client relationships" or "I energize teams") How might it hold you back? ("I avoid large meetings" or "I rush decisions.")

 **Partner with your opposite.** If you're inward-focused, team up with someone outward who brings momentum. If you're outward, pair with someone inward who thinks deeply. Same suit, different energy creates balance.

 **Adjust your environment.** Inward: Block solo work time. Outward: Schedule collaborative sessions. Design your day around your energy, not against it.

A

Inwardly
focused players
prefer depth
over breadth.
Outwardly focused
players feed off
energy and thrive
in groups.

Next Hand: *Now that you know the meaning of the 5 through Ace cards, in the next chapter, we'll dive into the 2, 3, and 4 cards—your strong suit gone wild.* →

CHAPTER 16

STRONG SUITS GONE WILD

When Your Personality Goes Too Far

In the previous chapter, we talked about the cards with the numbers 5 through Ace. Now it's time to dive into the 2, 3, and 4 cards—your strong suit on steroids.

Analytical and logical thinkers keep businesses on track. But when that strength turns into "know-it-all" behavior, you're probably not much fun at parties. That doesn't mean you should stifle that part of you.

A colleague, Alex, once admitted his natural style was a bit disorganized. For him, being a little scattered wasn't a flaw; it was his power. That's where his best ideas came from.

He knew it. Too much structure, and his creativity was stifled. Too little, and things fell apart.

His disorganization, when balanced, was a gift. However, when left unchecked, it became his Achilles heel.

That's what happens when strong suits go wild.

In Personality Poker, those are the cards with the numbers 2, 3, and 4. They represent your strong suit taken too far. Every suit has one.

Spades love facts and analysis. Taken too far? Analysis becomes paralysis. Decisions stall. Opportunities pass by. You become a know-it-all or skeptical.

Diamonds thrive on ideas and experiences. Taken too far? They chase every shiny object. Priorities blur. Energy scatters. Focus disappears and disorganization becomes the norm.

Clubs deliver results through planning. Taken too far? Structure strangles creativity. The checklist becomes a chokehold. Momentum stops and rigidity sets in.

Hearts connect with people. Taken too far? They avoid conflict. They smooth things over when tough calls are needed. They become overly sensitive or even self-sacrificing. Harmony wins while progress stalls.

The problem isn't the suit. It's the overuse.

A strong suit, pushed too far, becomes a liability.

But these overplayed suits aren't necessarily bad. It's part of who you are.

The difference between a Timex and a Rolex? It's the detail obsession of that "anal retentive" three of Clubs. Yes, that's an actual card in Personality Poker.

Alex's disorganization was a source of his creativity.

The trick is awareness. Notice when you've crossed the line. Ask teammates to flag you when you've gone too far.

And remember, sometimes the best way to manage your extremes is to let someone else step in with *their* strong suit.

PUT IT INTO PLAY

Your suit gone wild isn't necessarily bad; it's your strength pushed too far. The key is knowing when to pull back.

 **Identify when your strong suit goes too far.** Spades: analysis paralysis, skepticism. Diamonds: scattered focus, disorganization. Clubs: rigidity, over-control. Hearts: conflict avoidance, over-sensitivity.

 **Recall your last stuck moment.** Think about the last time you stalled at work. What caused it? Was it your strong suit taken too far?

 **Find your counterbalance.** Write down the name of someone whose strength is the antidote to your suit gone wild.

 **Create a signal.** Tell a trusted colleague: "When you see me doing [X behavior], call it out. I give you permission to say, 'Your strong suit has gone wild.'" Make it safe for them to flag you.

 **Embrace the gift of your wild side.** Alex's disorganization fueled his creativity. That wild side has value. Just don't let it run out of control. Notice when it's helping versus hurting.

Overplayed
suits aren't bad.
The difference
between a Timex
and a Rolex? A
detail-obsessed
perfectionist.

Next Hand: *Sometimes the real magic emerges from combinations. The next chapter explores what happens when two suits meet—and the superpowers that emerge when they do.* →

CHAPTER 17

When Two Suits are Better than One

Your Mix of Suits Defines Your Unique Superpower

Most people don't play with just one suit. You might be a Spade who's also part Club, or a Heart with a streak of Diamond. Those combinations matter. In addition to the numbers, they explain why two people with the same strong suit can feel completely different.

In Personality Poker, there are four common combinations. And they map directly to the real world.

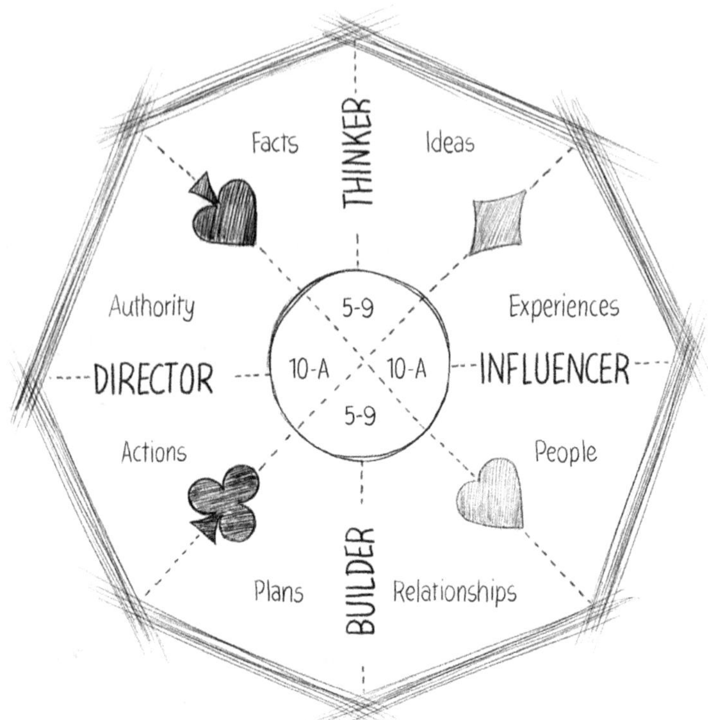

The Power of Combinations

Directors are Spades plus Clubs

Data plus discipline. Analysis plus execution. They've got the numbers, the process, and the drive to deliver. That's why so many CEOs of publicly traded companies land here.

It's the perfect combination. They're grounded in data and driven to act. Insight means nothing without results.

Builders are Clubs plus Hearts

Structure plus people. Actions plus empathy. These are the program and project managers. They keep the trains running on time and the passengers happy.

Their superpower is blending process and people. They build solid plans and motivate the teams who bring them to life.

Thinkers are Spades plus Diamonds

Logic plus creativity. Past plus future. They spot patterns in data while imagining new possibilities. They're the strategists who see what's coming next and can prove it.

They ground their vision in data while imagining new, different, and better futures.

Influencers are Diamonds plus Hearts

Not Instagram influencers. These are the real kind. They generate ideas and rally people around them. They're influential because their creativity excites people, and their relationships spread it.

The combination is what makes the difference.

Those are the most common combinations. However, when some people play, they end up with mainly Spades and Hearts or Clubs and Diamonds. Although these pairings occur, in many cases, these aren't true combinations but confusion between innate and learned strong suits. Remember Chapter 2?

Regardless, combinations matter. They give depth. They give context. They give you a role no single suit can deliver.

And the same is true for teams.

All **Directors**? You'll make progress, but not the right progress.
All **Builders**? Projects run smoothly, but the vision gets lost.
All **Thinkers**? Great strategies, but no movement.
All **Influencers**? Endless excitement but no follow-through.

Balance matters. And combinations are the glue.

So don't just ask, *"What's my strong suit?"* Ask, *"What's my combination hand?"* Because that's where your real role, and your real value, lives.

PUT IT INTO PLAY

Your combination, not just your suit, reveals your real power. Know it, name it, and fill the gaps on your team.

 **Identify your top two suits.** Look at your hand (or reflect on Chapters 1 and 2). Which two suits show up strongest for you? Write them down.

 **Name your combination.** Based on your top two suits, label yourself: Spades + Clubs = Director. Clubs + Hearts = Builder. Spades + Diamonds = Thinker. Diamonds + Hearts = Influencer.

 **Map your team's combinations.** Have each team member identify their top two suits and their combination type. Create a simple chart: Who's a Director? Builder? Thinker? Influencer?

 **Find the gap.** Look at your team map. Which combination is missing or underrepresented?

 **Hire or partner for the missing combination.** Actively seek someone who brings the combination your team lacks. Fill the gaps intentionally.

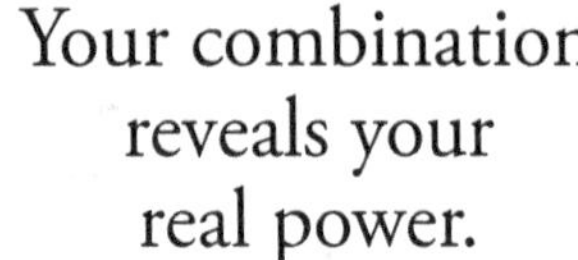

Next Hand: *Now for the bigger question: Who are we, really? The final chapter explores what changes over time, what doesn't, and how to play your truest game.* →

CHAPTER 18

WHO ARE WE REALLY?

Does Our Personality Change Over Time?

Somewhere along the way, most of us forget who we really are.

〰〰〰〰〰〰〰〰〰〰〰〰

After a Personality Poker session, I spoke with a man in his 60s, a semi-retired grandfather. He showed me his hand. All red cards.

He said, "If I had played this game twenty years ago, I would have picked mostly black cards."

He looked at me and asked, "Do people's personalities change?"

My answer comes from decades of watching thousands of people of all ages play this game.

As we explored in Chapter 7, the red cards represent creativity, connection, and play, while the black cards represent logic, structure, planning, and discipline.

When young children play Personality Poker, they almost always choose red cards. It's rare for them to pick cards about goals, structure, or expertise.

This makes sense. A NASA study by George Land found that 98 percent of five-year-olds test as highly creative. Kids are wired for play and connection—the red cards.

Then life happens. We go to school and learn to sit still, follow rules, and color inside the lines. Parents teach us to be practical. At work, we're rewarded for logic, order, and consistency.

Over time, we pick up more black cards. Not because that's who we are, but because that's what the world rewards. We learn to fit in and meet expectations—to please others instead of ourselves. But for many, something shifts later in life.

As the pressure to perform fades, many people start playing their red cards again. They spend more time with family and engage in philanthropic ventures.

The qualities that were always there finally have room to breathe.

I believe many of us, though not everyone, start life as red cards. That's our essence. The black cards help us succeed, but the red cards are who we've been all along.

Having said that, some individuals are genuinely black cards at their core. They should fully embrace that. Structure, logic, and discipline aren't constraints; they're strengths.

The point is, as we discussed in Chapter 2, embrace the real you.

Not the you you've become. Not the you you think you're supposed to be. The authentic you.

One color isn't better than the other. Both are needed to live a full, successful life.

If you feel like a red card at your core, don't wait until retirement to reclaim that part of yourself. Start playing your red cards now. Bring more creativity, connection, and play into your everyday life.

And if you're a black card who's been told to "loosen up" or "be more creative," stop apologizing for who you are. Your analytical mind and discipline are not limitations; they're your superpowers. Lean into them.

The goal isn't to change colors. It's to play your truest hand.

PUT IT INTO PLAY

Most of us shift over time between red and black cards. Life teaches us what's rewarded. The key is knowing which color feels natural and which feels learned.

 **Check your current color balance.** Look at your hand or reflect on recent behavior. Are you playing mostly red (creative, relational, playful) or black (logical, structured, disciplined) right now?

 **Ask: Which feels natural versus learned?** One color might be your essence. The other might be what you've adapted to survive. Write down which feels like "home" and which feels like "work."

 **Find the shift point (if there was one).** Did you start playing a different color at school? Your first job? A specific role? Some people stay consistent their whole lives. Others shift. Both are valid.

 **Reclaim what's missing.** If you've lost your red side, add creativity and connection to your daily routine. If you've suppressed your black side, build in structure, analysis, or planning. Start small. Start today. Don't wait for retirement to reclaim the real you.

 **Balance, don't choose.** You need both colors to live fully. The goal isn't to pick one—it's to honor what's natural while developing what's needed.

Embrace the real you. Not the you you've become or think you are supposed to be— the authentic you. The goal isn't to change colors. It's to play your truest hand.

Next Hand: *You've learned to play the game. Now it's time to explore the Wild Cards. This is where science, experience, and AI join the table.* →

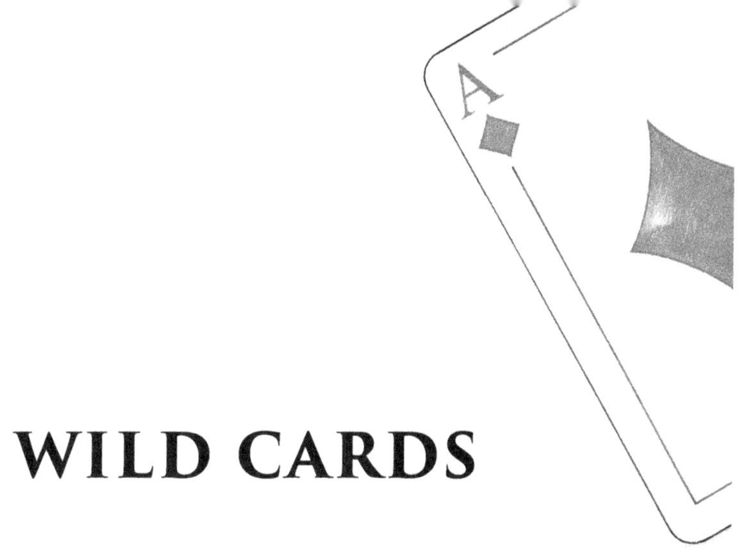

WILD CARDS

Further Thoughts

Every game has its surprises. Personality Poker is no different.

Wild Cards are the ideas that don't fit neatly into any one suit but can change how you view the game.

In this section, we'll look at how Personality Poker connects to research and real-world results, why blending different experiences multiplies breakthroughs, and where the game goes next given the world of AI.

Think of this part as the bonus hand. The one that helps you see the bigger picture and play with even more intention.

Because every great player knows that the wild cards are the ones that change everything.

THE SCIENCE OF PERSONALITY POKER

It's Not Just Fun and Games

When I first created the Personality Poker game in 2005, I came up with fifty-two words that I thought matched each style.

For example, I guessed that "nurturing" would belong to the Hearts and "creative" would map to Diamonds.

But they were only guesses.

In 2009, Penguin Portfolio bought the rights to the Personality Poker book. By then, more than twenty thousand people around the world had already played the game. I knew it worked. But the Spade in me couldn't help but wonder: Is it actually valid?

Do the words really measure what they're supposed to measure?

To validate the system, I reached out to Michael Wiederman, a psychology professor at Columbia College in South Carolina and an expert in psychological testing.

I told him that Personality Poker was simple but surprisingly insightful. It gave deep understanding in minutes while being fun and intuitive.

But I wondered if something this simple could really be scientifically sound.

Michael smiled. "Simple is good," he said. "And there's a difference between being valid and being useful."

He told me about a study that compared several complex depression tests to one simple question: Are you depressed? Despite all the formulas and statistics, none of the fancy tests performed significantly better than that one question.

In practice, the tests were statistically valid but complicated to administer. The simple question proved more practical and useful.

I wanted both: usefulness and validity. With Michael's help, we put Personality Poker to the test.

We built surveys to validate it statistically. Starting with more than a hundred descriptive words, we asked over two hundred people to choose the ones that best described them. Then we ran the numbers to see which words connected most strongly to each style.

I secretly hoped the results would line up perfectly: four styles, fifty-two words.

But that's not what happened.

Most people didn't fit neatly into one suit. They showed a mix of styles.

At first, that felt like a flaw. Then I realized: that's real life.

People aren't one-dimensional. They're a blend of strengths and styles. And that's what makes Personality Poker work.

It's not just about accuracy. It's about awareness.

The real magic happens in the conversations the cards create. People start seeing themselves and others differently. Insights emerge that no standard test could reveal.

The idea of using cards for the assessment didn't appear by accident. It's rooted in proven research.

Personality Poker is based on a method called a Q-sort, developed by psychologist William Stephenson in 1953. It's a proven way to explore how people perceive themselves and those around them.

In a Q-sort, people sort cards or statements to show how well they fit. That same approach became the foundation for Personality Poker.

Later, I partnered with Harvard University to create an online version. Although the technology eventually aged out, this work tested players' beliefs at a deeper level, further validating our approach.

The system worked.

So don't let the simplicity fool you. Personality Poker gives you a fast, accurate way to see how you and others think.

It's a mirror. It's a conversation starter. And it just happens to be a lot of fun to play.

A

It's not just about accuracy, it's about awareness. The real magic happens in the conversations the cards create.

PLAYING WITH A FULL DECK OF EXPERIENCES

Why Personality Diversity Is Not Enough

Playing with a full deck isn't just about personalities. It's also about experiences. When you blend both purposefully, breakthroughs multiply.

The four suits tell you how people think. But what they've done shapes what they bring to the table.

A Diamond who's lived in five countries connects different dots than a Diamond who's never left their hometown.

A Spade with a PhD in physics asks different questions than a Spade with an MBA.

A Club who served in the military executes differently than a Club who built startups.

A Heart who was a social worker understands people differently than a Heart who led customer success teams.

Same suit. Different lens.

When Different Worlds Collide

Each year, an event called Pumps and Pipes brings together cardiologists and oil industry engineers to discuss problems related to fluids moving through tubes. Blood in arteries, oil in pipelines.

One breakthrough was the Greenfield inferior vena cava filter, a medical device that traps blood clots before they reach the lungs. The cardiologist who invented it got the idea from a pipeline engineer who created filters that remove sludge from oil pipelines.

Another was a cardiologist who helped a gas company develop a self-sealing system for pipelines by studying how blood clots. They built a system that automatically finds and seals cracks the way the human body does.

Different industries. Shared problems. Fresh solutions.

Both groups had the same suits. But their different experiences gave them different dots to connect.

The Dots You Have to Connect

A potato chip manufacturer wanted to shake excess oil off chips without breaking them. Every vibrating machine they tried shattered the chips.

The solution came from someone outside the food industry: a musician who played the bass guitar.

He realized that when he played, nearby objects vibrated without breaking. So he placed chips on a rack under a loudspeaker and adjusted the frequency and volume until they vibrated just enough to shed oil, without shattering.

He was probably a Diamond. But what mattered more was that he had dots no one else in the room had. Years of making strings vibrate gave him visceral knowledge of frequency and resonance.

The Diamonds on the engineering team were just as creative. But they only had engineering dots to connect.

The bass player had music dots. That made all the difference.

Why Expertise Can Blind You

Harvard professor Lee Fleming analyzed 17,000 patents and found that teams with similar backgrounds delivered steady and predictable improvements.

But the most valuable innovations came from groups with diverse experiences. They produced ideas no single discipline could reach alone.

A team of four Diamonds will generate creative ideas. But if all four have the same background, they'll connect the same dots.

Put a Diamond engineer with a Diamond musician, teacher, or chef, and now you're connecting dots across different universes.

Similarity breeds efficiency. Diversity breeds discovery.

If your team feels stuck, don't just check for all four suits. Ask what experiences are missing.

Instead of only hiring from within your industry, bring in an outsider.

If your team has been together for years, invite someone who hasn't learned "how things work here."

Every new lens adds new dots to connect.

The Real Game

Personality tells you how someone thinks. Experience tells you what they've learned to see.

You need both.

A full deck of personalities without diverse experiences means you're balanced but playing small. A full deck of experiences without personality diversity leaves gaps in the innovation process.

The magic happens when you have both. When your Spades come from different fields. When your Diamonds have lived different lives. When your Clubs learned execution in different environments. When your Hearts have built relationships in different cultures.

So when building your next team, resist only hiring people who look like they belong.

The person you need most might be the one whose résumé makes no sense.

Play with a full deck of personalities.

And play with a full deck of experiences.

That's how you win big.

A

A full deck of
personalities without
diverse experiences
means you're balanced
but playing small.
A full deck of
experiences without
personality diversity
leaves gaps in the
innovation process. 

Playing with AI

Why the More Digital We Get, the More Human We Must Become

Artificial intelligence is changing everything. It can out-analyze any Spade, out-execute any Club, and out-ideate any Diamond.

But it can't do one thing: be human.

As technology advances, our advantage shifts from what we know to how we think, connect, and create.

The skills that made us valuable yesterday—processing information, following procedures, generating ideas—are now commoditized by machines.

If AI represents the ultimate logic machine, then humans must become the ultimate meaning makers.

The Four Suits in an AI World

To thrive in an age of algorithms, we need to double down on our four suits—but in ways that complement AI, not compete with it.

Spades ask better questions.

AI can analyze anything, but it can't determine what's worth analyzing.

The right questions are critical in an age of AI. Ask the wrong question and you'll get a precise answer to the wrong problem.

The future belongs to those who think critically about what matters, not just those who compute quickly.

Spades define the problem. AI solves it.

Clubs implement with judgment.

AI can execute processes, but it can't navigate the messy human reality of implementation.

Ideas have no impact without follow-through, discipline, and the wisdom to know when to adapt. Clubs convert digital concepts into physical realities, making judgment calls that no algorithm can make.

Diamonds build bridges across disciplines.

AI draws from its training data, but it can't make the creative leaps that come from lived experience.

Diamonds connect dots others don't see, finding intersections between unrelated fields that technology can't replicate. They ask "What if?" in ways that challenge assumptions, not just optimize existing patterns.

Hearts engage people in new ways.

In a world where digital capability is rapidly becoming a commodity, the only true differentiator for an organization is its people.

Hearts bring empathy and connection to the center of innovation. They build the trust, alignment, and human connection that makes change possible.

AI can't persuade. It can't inspire. It can't make someone feel understood.

The Human Advantage

AI can play the game faster. But we play it smarter, deeper, and with purpose.

It can process. We can discern.
It can optimize. We can imagine.
It can execute. We can adapt.
It can inform. We can inspire.

As the world becomes more digital, our value lies in what makes us human. The ability to ask questions that matter. The judgment to know when the rules don't apply. The creativity to see what doesn't yet exist. The empathy to bring people along.

So as we build the future with machines, remember: The winning hand isn't artificial. It's human.

And it's playing with a full deck.

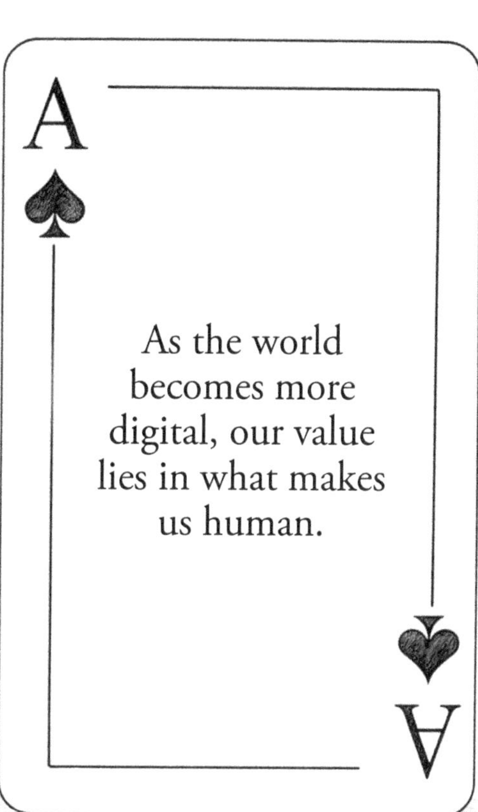

A
As the world
becomes more
digital, our value
lies in what makes
us human.

PLAYING THE WHOLE GAME

How to Win with a Full Deck

You've learned how to play with a full deck. Now it's time to put it into practice.

Most people stop here. They read, they nod, they move on.

But transformation doesn't happen from insight alone. It happens when you actually use what you've learned.

This chapter gives you a 14-day plan to make it real and shows you how to handle the roadblocks you may face.

THE 14-DAY PLAYBOOK

This plan follows a proven sequence: know yourself → understand others → map the team → take action → build new habits.

You can adapt it to your situation, but the order matters. Each step builds on the one before it.

Days 1–2: Name Your Hand

Self-awareness

Play the game using cards or the online version. Lock in your top five cards. Share them with your team.

No cards? Write down your top five traits.

Days 3–4: See What Others See

External perspective

Ask a trusted colleague if they agree with your hand.

Then run a gifting session with your team. Give each other cards based on what everyone observes, and discuss the differences between how you see yourselves and how others see you.

Listen. Don't defend.

No cards? Just share stories that provide perspective.

Days 5–6: Map the Table

Team diagnosis

Create a one-page team map. List everyone's primary and secondary suits. Highlight the gaps. Which suits are missing or underrepresented? How can you close those gaps?

Days 7–8: Pair the Opposites

Creative conflict

Create at least two "Ray & Steve" pairs for your current priorities. Match a Spade with a Heart, or a Diamond with a Club.

Give them a shared goal and simple rules of engagement: "We'll disagree on approach, not on outcomes."

Practice. Observe. Learn.

Days 9–10: Deal Out the Work

Strategic assignment

For your next project, assign suit-fit roles. Post who's framing and analyzing (Spades), creating and envisioning (Diamonds), planning and executing (Clubs), and engaging and connecting (Hearts).

Make it visible so everyone knows their role.

Day 11: Run a Meeting by Suit

Structured inclusion

Optimize your next meeting:

- Ask, "What suit is this meeting?" (Data review? Brainstorm? Status update? Team check-in?).
- Find a meeting leader who has that suit.
- Have the leader invite other suits to help design the meeting.
- Run it so every suit gets airtime and no one dominates.
- Track your meeting portfolio and make sure you're not running the same type on repeat.

Day 12: Praise by Suit

Recognition

To create a culture of innovation, every suit needs to be valued:

- Recognize one person every day for what they bring to the table.
- Praise them the way *they* want to be praised, not the standard way.
- Identify what's undervalued and publicly appreciate those contributions.

Day 13: Shuffle Once

Perspective shift

Swap one role for a week to spark fresh thinking. Have a Diamond lead a status meeting. Let a Club run a brainstorm. Ask a Spade to lead a team-building session. Put a Heart in charge of data analysis. Capture what you learn about how others experience the work.

Create appreciation and empathy for what others contribute.

Day 14 and Beyond: Set the Rules, Not Just the Roles

Sustainable culture

Culture requires that all suits be valued and appreciated. Environment alignment beats task assignment every time. People thrive when the rules match their style:

- Be sure to value all suits. Adjust your performance management guidelines to acknowledge all the suits.
- Assign based on environment, not task. Put black cards in structured situations and red cards in ambiguous ones.
- Hire for what's missing. When adding to your team, ask: "Who do we need that we may not have hired in the past?"
- Review monthly.

When You Get Stuck

Even the best plans hit roadblocks. Here's how to handle the most common ones.

"I don't have access to the cards."
You don't need them. Just ask people to name their top five traits or describe how they think. The conversations matter more than the cards.

"We've already done personality tests. How is this different?"
Personality Poker isn't just another assessment. Most tools tell you about individuals. This one diagnoses teams and organizations. It shows you what's missing, who you need, and how to work better together. Use it in meetings, hiring decisions, and project assignments. It's not a one-time test—it's a working language for collaboration.

"My team thinks this is silly."
Some people see personality work as "fluffy." Don't lead with the game or personalities. Lead with the business problem

your team faces: missed deadlines, stalled innovation, poor collaboration. Then show how balance solves it.

"We're all the same suit."
Start by acknowledging it: "We're all Clubs. That's why we execute well but struggle with creativity." Then deliberately bring in a Diamond for your next project. Test it out. Prove the value before asking for permanent change.

"I tried pairing opposites and they clashed."
That's normal. The first time opposites work together, tension is high. Give them a shared goal, clear rules of engagement, and time. And make sure they have the tools to appreciate what each brings to the table. The magic happens after they learn each other's language.

"Someone was offended by the cards they received."
Gifting can trigger defensiveness if not handled carefully. In some environments, it's safer not to allow the 2, 3, and 4 cards to be gifted to others. Frame receiving cards as data, not judgment. It's about perceived behavior, not character. Make it safe to be surprised.

YOUR MOVE

You've got the plan. Now it's your turn to deal.

The next time someone drives you crazy, pause. They might be the card you've been missing. Like Ray was for me, they may be the person who saves your career.

Play big. Play bold. Play with a full deck.

Play It Forward

How to Keep the Momentum Going and Drive Results

You've learned how to play with a full deck. You've seen how different styles shape innovation, teamwork, and leadership.

Now it's time to take the next step—from awareness to mastery.

There are three ways to double down and bring Personality Poker deeper into your work.

1. DIY (Do It Yourself)

Want to play Personality Poker with your team? Start here.

DIY System: Get five decks of specially designed Personality Poker cards, a quick-start guide, instructional videos, PowerPoint slides, templates, and everything you need to run sessions immediately. You don't need certification to make an impact—just curiosity and a willingness to play.

It is fast, fun, and remarkably insightful. Use them in meetings, workshops, or leadership retreats.

Order at PersonalityPokerStore.com

2. Enterprise Solutions: Licensing, Certification, and Mastery

Ready to bring Personality Poker into your organization at scale? We offer three levels designed to embed this framework into your culture.

Licensing gives your entire organization access to video-based training, digital tools, live webinars, and physical card decks so everyone can start playing with a full deck immediately.

Certification takes it deeper. Your internal facilitators learn to run powerful sessions that drive measurable business results. Use them for leadership development, innovation programs, team diagnostics, and culture transformation.

Mastery is for organizations going all in. Your leaders explore advanced frameworks for collaboration and culture change, learning how to embed Personality Poker into your DNA. It's not just about playing the game—it's about reshaping how your organization thinks, leads, and grows.

Join a global community of practitioners transforming how teams work and win together.

Learn more: PersonalityPokerMastery.com

3. Keynotes and Workshops

Looking to transform your next event into an interactive experience?

Bring me to your event and I'll deliver one of the most engaging keynotes your audience will experience.

They will learn how to spot the missing cards, build balanced teams, and design for healthy conflict that drives innovation—all in as little as one hour.

Perfect for:

- Leadership offsites
- Annual conferences
- Team kickoffs
- Strategy workshops
- Team-building retreats
- Innovation summits

Your audience will leave with actionable insights and a fresh perspective on the people who drive them crazy.

Want to see what it looks like in action? Go to *PersonalityPokerVideo.com* to watch a three-minute video.

Learn more about speeches at: PersonalityPoker.com

Whether you start with the online game, the DIY system, or a deep dive into Mastery, you're already part of something bigger.

You're building teams that celebrate difference, cultures that embrace collaboration, and leaders who play to win—together.

Now it's your turn to deal the next hand.

Play smart. Play full out.

And play with a full deck.

I'd love to hear how this book and the cards change the game for you. What did you learn about yourself or your team? What breakthrough did you have about a colleague who used to drive you crazy, or what questions are you wrestling with as you put this into practice? I read and respond to every message, and your stories make this work better.

And if you found value here, **consider leaving an honest review**. This will help others discover their full deck.

Stephen Shapiro
steve@personalitypoker.com

About the Author

Hi, I'm Stephen Shapiro.

Early in my career, I believed efficiency was everything.

I studied Industrial Engineering at Cornell University and became a process improvement consultant at Accenture, helping companies streamline operations and cut costs.

Then one project changed everything—it was designed to eliminate 10,000 jobs.

That's when it hit me: whenever we optimized a company's processes, they downsized the workforce. Real people with families and dreams.

From that moment, I made a promise. I would never again be responsible for a lost job. Instead of helping companies shrink, I would help them grow through innovation.

Soon after, I built and led a 20,000-person process and innovation practice at Accenture that helped people focus on value creation rather than software implementation.

Since then, I've spent my career helping organizations unlock that difference. I've written eight books, including this one, all focused on one goal: making innovation practical, human, and a little more fun.

More than 250,000 people around the world have played Personality Poker. I've shared my innovation ideas on stages in over fifty countries and on television networks like ABC, CNBC, USA, and TLC.

When I'm not speaking or writing, you can find me practicing magic or playing my saxophone. Magic is about making the seemingly impossible possible. Improvisational jazz creates something new in the moment. Both are perfect metaphors for innovation.

Along the way, I've been honored to be inducted into the Speaker Hall of Fame and to serve as a Senior Research Fellow with The Conference Board.

Thirty years after that project where 10,000 people lost their jobs, my mission of growth still drives me.

And one of the keys to growth is making sure you, your team, and your organization are playing with a full deck.

FURTHER READING

Research Studies and Additional Information

I love some good Spade analysis. If you want to dig deeper into any of these topics, here are some of the research studies I used in writing the original Personality Poker book, written in 2010, and referenced in this one.

Chapter 2

Learned vs natural strengths: Biswas-Diener, Robert. "Learned Behaviors Are Not Strengths!" Unavailable article, formerly published online.

Chapter 5

Self-perception vs the perception of others: Grucza, Richard A., and Lewis R. Goldberg. "The Comparative Validity of Eleven Modern Personality Inventories: Predictions of Behavioral Acts, Informant Reports, and Clinical Indicators." *Journal of Personality Assessment* 89, no. 2 (2007): 167–187.

Chapter 6

New Zealand medical teams: McCallin, Antoinette, and Anita Bamford. "Interdisciplinary Teamwork: Is the Influence of Emotional Intelligence Fully Appreciated?" *Journal of Nursing Management* 15 (2007): 386–391.

Hiring in pairs: Mieszkowski, Katherine. "Opposites Attract." *Fast Company*, December 31, 1997.

Why Hiring Focused on People Who Fit the Mold: Coutu, Diane. "Why Teams DON'T Work" (interview with J. Richard Hackman). *Harvard Business Review*, May 2009.

Chapter 7

Debunking the left-brain and right-brain myth: Lilienfeld, Scott O., Steven Jay Lynn, John Ruscio, and Barry L. Beyerstein. *50 Great Myths of Popular Psychology: Shattering Widespread Misconceptions about Human Behavior.* Chichester, West Sussex, and Malden, MA: Wiley-Blackwell, 2009.

Why We Use Our Whole Brain: Hellige, Joseph B. "Unity of Thought and Action: Varieties of Interaction Between the Left and Right Cerebral Hemispheres." *Current Directions in Psychological Science* 2, no. 21 (1993).

The Value of Line Thinking in Innovation: Post, Corinne, Emilio De Lia, Nancy DiTomaso, Thomas M. Tirpak, and Rajendra Borwankar. "Capitalizing on Thought Diversity for Innovation." Research Technology Management, November 1, 2009.

Steve Jobs quote: Wolf, Gary. "The Next Insanely Great Thing."

Wired, February 1, 1996. *https://www.wired.com/1996/02/jobs-2/*.

Chapter 8

Why rules matter more than roles: Hammerschmidt, Peter K. "The Kirton Adaption-Innovation Inventory and Group Problem Solving Success Rates." *Journal of Creative Behavior* 30, no. 1 (1996).

Chapter 9

Homogeneous team effectiveness: Bowers, Clint A., James A. Pharmer, and Eduardo Salas. "When Member Homogeneity Is Needed in Work Teams: A Meta-Analysis." *Small Group Research* 31 (2000): 305–327.

Wharton study on diversity: Barsade, Sigal, Andrew J. Ward, Jeanne M. Turner, and Jeffrey A. Sonnenfeld. "To Your Heart's Content: A Model of Affective Diversity in Top Management Teams." *Administrative Science Quarterly* 45 (2000): 802–836.

Chapter 11

Kirton's cognitive climate research: Kirton, M. J., and R. M. McCarthy. "Cognitive Climate and Organizations." *Journal of Occupational Psychology* 61 (1988): 175–184.

Chapter 13

Aristotle's rhetorical triangle: Sichach, Moses. "Ethos, Pathos, and Logos as Foundations of Persuasive Writing." September 4, 2024. SSRN. *https://ssrn.com/abstract=4971293*.

Chapter 16

Why creative people are messier: "Say Yes to Mess." *New York Times*, December 21, 2006. *http://www.nytimes.com/2006/12/21/garden/21mess.html*.

Chapter 18

Why kids are more creative: Land, George, and Beth Jarman. NASA creativity test results as described in *Breakpoint and Beyond: Mastering the Future Today*. San Francisco, CA: HarperBusiness, 1993.

The Science of Personality Poker

Q-sort methodology overview: "Q-Sort." Wikipedia. *https://en.wikipedia.org/wiki/Q_methodology*.

Playing with a Full Deck of Experiences

The Harvard Study: Fleming, Lee. "Perfecting Cross-Pollination." *Harvard Business Review* 82, no. 9 (September 2004): 22-24.